Ensemble Machine Learning

超実践
アンサンブル機械学習

武藤佳恭 著

近代科学社

◆ 読者の皆さまへ ◆

　平素より，小社の出版物をご愛読くださいまして，まことに有り難うございます．

　㈱近代科学社は 1959 年の創立以来，微力ながら出版の立場から科学・工学の発展に寄与すべく尽力してきております．それも，ひとえに皆さまの温かいご支援があってのものと存じ，ここに衷心より御礼申し上げます．

　なお，小社では，全出版物に対して HCD（人間中心設計）のコンセプトに基づき，そのユーザビリティを追求しております．本書を通じまして何かお気づきの事柄がございましたら，ぜひ以下の「お問合せ先」までご一報くださいますよう，お願いいたします．

　お問合せ先：reader@kindaikagaku.co.jp

　なお，本書の制作には，以下が各プロセスに関与いたしました：

- 企画：小山　透
- 編集：高山哲司，安原悦子
- 組版：加藤文明社（LaTeX）
- 印刷：加藤文明社
- 製本：加藤文明社（PUR）
- 資材管理：加藤文明社
- カバー・表紙デザイン：加藤文明社
- 広報宣伝・営業：山口幸治，冨髙琢磨，西村知也

本書に記載されている会社名・製品名等は，一般に各社の登録商標または商標です．本文中の ©，®，™ 等の表示は省略しています．

・本書の複製権・翻訳権・譲渡権は株式会社近代科学社が保有します．
・ JCOPY 〈(社)出版者著作権管理機構 委託出版物〉
本書の無断複写は著作権法上での例外を除き禁じられています．
複写される場合は，そのつど事前に(社)出版者著作権管理機構
（電話 03-3513-6969，FAX 03-3513-6979，e-mail: info@jcopy.or.jp）の
許諾を得てください．

はじめに

　近年，オープンソースの急速な発達が，機械学習の分野に大きな進歩をもたらしています．いつのまにか，オープンソースの製品が読者諸氏の身の回りにも多数存在するようになったと思います．例えば，皆さんが日常使っているスマートフォンの多くは，Google 社の Android か Apple 社の iPhone のいずれかでしょう．実は，両方のスマートフォンとも，Linux や Unix-like の OS をベースに構築されているオープンソースの製品なのです．

　日本では，オープンソースの信頼性に疑いを持つ企業がありますが，企業の幹部は，本人も含めて，その企業に在籍する社員のほとんどがオープンソースのスマートフォンを利用していることを理解していないようです．

　現在のソフトウェア開発で重要なことは，オープンソースのようにプログラムソースを公開することであり，このことが，信頼性の裏づけ，ひいては危険回避につながるということです．逆に，クローズソースの場合は，プログラムがブラックボックスとなり，予想できない事態が起こる可能性があります．特に，自動運転などの人命に関わる分野では，クローズソースの危険性・信頼性をもう一度見直す必要があります．クローズソースのハードウェアも同様の問題を抱えています[*]．

　オープンソースのもう 1 つの利点は，オリジナルソースに変更を加えて，性能向上を図ったり，新機能を加えたりすることが可能になることです．この特徴は，「incremental revolution」と呼ばれています．

　本書では，Python 言語を活用して機械学習を説明していきます[**]．オープンソースの scikit-learn(sklearn) ライブラリや statsmodels ライブラリを利用します．Python には多くの役に立つライブラリがあり，簡単にそれらのライブラリを活用できます．

　本書ではまず，皆さんのパソコン上にオープンソース機械学習のための開発環境を構築します．機械学習を理解するために，多くの事例を示し，そのプログラムを読者諸氏が試せるようにしています．

　つまり，パソコン上で，さまざまなアルゴリズムを試しながら，機械学習を体験できるようにしました．どのプログラムも極めて短いので，理解でき

---

[*] 自動車における，オープンソースとクローズソースの問題点に関しては，付録（*Science* 誌に掲載された eLetters）を参照してください．読者諸氏の分野でも，クローズソースの問題が必ずあると思われます．

[**] 本書は，Python 2.7.12 での動作確認を行ったうえで執筆しました．後継バージョンでは，操作や結果が異なる場合があります．

るようになるのに，それほど時間はかからないと思います．難しい理論が理解できなくても，オープンソースのライブラリの活用ができるようになることが，本書の目的です．習うより慣れろの考え方を踏まえて，できるだけ実例を多く示し，読者が理解できるようにしました．

本書では，すべてのプログラムソースコードを公開しているので，どの部分でも変更可能です．つまり，皆さんが，自らのデータセットを用意さえすれば，プログラム変更なしで（データを取り扱うプログラムコードを除く：3行），ビッグデータ解析・予測が可能になります．

本書でのビッグデータ分析とは，"正確な予測"，"データモデルの自動構築"，"データの自動特徴分析" の3つです．

歴史的には，本書の重要なキーワードである機械学習の分野も紆余曲折の道を歩んできています．機械学習の分野というのは，コンピュータサイエンスの一分野ですが，その機械学習を支えてきた人工知能 (AI) は，論理学 (logic) によって長い間発展してきました．日本では，政府が支援した第五世代プロジェクトにおいて，その述語論理（論理学）をベースに優秀な人工知能を構築しようという目論見でした．

ここで新たに浮上してきた技術が，一時見放されていた，人工脳神経回路モデル（ニューラルネット）の研究分野です．いま，ニューラルネットの研究分野が復活を果たしています．ニューラルネットモデルをベースに，再び人工知能を構築しようとする新たな試みが始まりました．著者も，1989年にニューラルネットモデルを使って，*Science* 誌に論文を発表しました (http://science.sciencemag.org/content/245/4923/1221)．

また，1992年に，高速に機械学習できる，Functional-Link net を *IEEE Computer* 誌に発表しました (http://ieeexplore.ieee.org/xpl/articleDetails.jsp?reload=true&arnumber=144401)．

現在の人工知能技術は，ニューラルネットや最先端統計学が融合した技術へと急速に発展してきています．

いま流行のディープラーニング（深層学習）はまさに，ニューラルネット技術が急成長した姿であり，名前を変えて再デビューを果たしています．ディープラーニングでは，CPU だけでなく GPU を効率よく利用して大規模な機械学習が可能になりました．その大規模 GPU 機械学習が，人工知能の分野で主流になってきています．

1つの CPU ではせいぜい複数個のコアですが，GPU では数千個以上のコアが1チップに内蔵され，しかも安価に購入できます．実は GPU は機械学習

のために作られてきたものではなく，ゲーム用のビデオ分野から成長してきました．GPUメーカとして有名なのが，NVIDIA社です．そのGPUを使って，超並列な機械学習が可能となりました．

人工知能技術は目覚ましく発展し，世界では，チェス世界チャンピオンを打ち負かし，将棋のプロ棋士に勝利を収め，最近では，世界囲碁チャンピオンに勝利しています．

本書では，赤ワインの人工ソムリエを構築しました．赤ワインの品質を判断するシステムで，なんと正答率が77％に到達し，人間のソムリエに勝つのではないかと思われます．人間と違って機械は酔っ払わないので，何万時間でも，休むことなくワインの正確な品質判断の作業がリアルタイムにできます．

機械学習の分野には，機械学習した既知の特性からデータ予測する分野と，データから未知の情報を発見するデータマイニングの分野の2つがあります．本書では，前者の分野に焦点を絞り，ビッグデータ解析に活用できるように説明していきます．また，前者の分野が後者のデータマイニングの分野にも，深く影響しているので，本書で紹介する機械学習の手法は，データマイニングにも応用可能です．

本書では，ビッグデータ解析のために，統計学分野の重回帰分析手法を説明します．重回帰分析には，最小二乗法OLS，一般化最小二乗法GLS，加重最小二乗法WLS，ロバスト線形モデルRLM，Lasso線形モデル，自己相関付き実行可能一般化最小二乗法GLSAR，混合線形モデルMixedLM，分位点回帰QuantReg，OMP手法，イラスティックネットElasticNetなどがあります．

重回帰分析では，重回帰式モデルを我々人間が考案作成しなくてはいけません．つまり，従来の重回帰分析に頼る限り，ビッグデータ解析では，かなりの専門知識が必要になります．

本書で紹介する機械学習では，機械学習器にデータを与えることにより，自動的にモデル構築・生成できます．つまり，ビッグデータ解析では，機械学習の手法を使うことで，人間がモデルを作成する必要がなくなったのです．つまり，専門知識なしでも，機械学習を用いれば，ビッグデータ解析ができる時代が到来したということです．

本書では，最高気温や店の前の通行人数が，アイスクリームの売上げにどのように影響するのか，31日分のデータを分析し，売上げ予測をします．

機械学習に関しては，サポートベクトル回帰SVR，カーネルリッジ回帰KRR，

ナイーブ・ベイズ (GaussianNB, MultinomialNB, BernoulliNB)，決定木分類器 DecisionTreeClassifier，3 つの近傍法 (KNeighborsRegressor, KNeighborsClassifier, RadiusNeighborsClassifier)，確率的勾配降下法 SGDClassifier，ディープラーニングニューラルネットワーク keras などを紹介します．

さらに，本書では，複数の機械学習器や分類器をアンサンブルできる，アンサンブル学習を紹介します．アンサンブル学習では，アダブースト (Adaboost)，ランダムフォーレスト (RandomForest)，エキストラツリー (ExtraTree)，エキストラツリーズ (ExtraTrees)，グラディエントブースティング (GradientBoosting)，バッギング (Bagging)，多数決分類器 (VotingClassifier) などの 7 つの手法を紹介します．

第 4 章では，応用例として，クレジットカードのデフォルトの学習と赤ワインの品質を判別できる人工ソムリエの 2 つを紹介します．決まりきった専門業務であればあるほど，人間の仕事は人工知能に簡単に置き換わっていきます．これからの社会を考えると，子供の教育の考え方を大きく変えなくてはいけません．なぜならば，子供が願った多くの仕事が，近い将来なくなる可能性があるからです．

第 5 章では，最近，囲碁チャンピオンを破った AlphaGo が使っている，畳み込みニューラルネットワークを紹介します．最新の画像認識技術が AlphaGo で活用されました．画風も棋風 (碁風) も同様に扱える時代になりました．画像認識技術は，文書処理にも現在応用されています．ここでは，深層ニューラルネットワークライブラリ (chainer と keras) とオープンソース画像処理ライブラリ OpenCV を活用して，写真画像から有名画家風の絵画を生成します．

本書で紹介する実例を参考にしながら，問題にチャレンジしてください．新しい問題にチャレンジするには，ビッグデータ分析に必要なデータの収集が一番難しい作業になります．

新しい成果が出たら，ぜひ，著者に報告してください．皆さんの成果を楽しみにしています．

2016 年 11 月
武藤佳恭

はじめに vii

---

keywords

オープンソース，クローズソース，人工知能，AI，ビッグデータ，重回帰分析，重回帰式，最小二乗法 OLS，一般化最小二乗法 GLS，加重最小二乗法 WLS，ロバスト線形モデル RLM，Lasso 線形モデル，自己相関付き実行可能一般化最小二乗法 GLSAR，混合線形モデル MixedLM，分位点回帰 QuantReg，OMP 手法，イラスティック・ネット ElasticNet，機械学習，サポートベクトル回帰 SVR，カーネルリッジ回帰 KRR，ナイーブ・ベイズ (GaussianNB, MultinomialNB, BernoulliNB)，決定木分類器 DecisionTreeClassifier，近傍法 (KNeighborsRegressor, KNeighborsClassifier, RadiusNeighborsClassifier)，確率的勾配降下法 SGDClassifier，ディープラーニングニューラルネットワーク keras，人工ソムリエ，クレジットカードのデフォルト，Python，アンサンブル機械学習，アダブースト (Adaboost)，ランダムフォーレスト (RandomForest)，エキストラツリー (ExtraTree)，エキストラツリーズ (ExtraTrees)，グラディエントブースティング (GradientBoosting)，バッギング (Bagging)，多数決分類器 (Voting)，畳み込みニューラルネットワーク

本書をお読みになる前に

本書では，機械学習を体験していただくための実行環境の設定や，さまざまなプログラム・ファイルの実行手順などについて解説しています．これらは計算環境によってはリスクを伴います．これらの操作で生じたいかなるトラブルに対しても，著者ならびに㈱近代科学社は一切の責任を負いかねます．読者のみなさまの自己責任で行っていただくようお願いいたします．あらかじめ，ご了承ください．

目次

はじめに iii

第 0 章　機械学習の基礎と環境設定　　　　　　　　　1

0.0　機械学習とは 1
0.1　機械学習実行環境設定 2
　　0.1.0　Windows 上で直接実行できる環境構築 3
　　0.1.1　Linux 上で実行できる環境構築 9
　　0.1.2　Ubuntu を Windows 10 上で直接動作させる .. 11

第 1 章　ビッグデータ解析と機械学習　　　　　　　　15

1.0　ビッグデータ解析とは 15
1.1　重回帰分析とは 16
　　1.1.0　最小二乗法 OLS 17
　　1.1.1　一般化最小二乗法 GLS 24
　　1.1.2　加重最小二乗法 WLS 24
　　1.1.3　ロバスト線形モデル RLM 25
　　1.1.4　Lasso 線形モデル 27

1.1.5 自己相関付き実行可能一般化最小二乗法 GLSAR 28
1.1.6 混合線形モデル MixedLM 29
1.1.7 分位点回帰 QuantReg 30
1.1.8 OMP 手法 31
1.1.9 イラスティックネット ElasticNet 32

第2章 機械学習 35

2.0 サポートベクトル回帰 SVR 36
2.1 カーネルリッジ回帰 KRR 37
2.2 ナイーブ・ベイズ sklearn.naive_bayes 機械学習 38
2.3 決定木分類器 DecisionTreeClassifier 41
2.4 近傍法 42
2.5 確率的勾配降下法 SGDClassifier 44
2.6 ディープラーニングニューラルネットワーク keras ... 45

第3章 アンサンブル機械学習 51

3.0 アダブースト (Adaboost) 51
3.1 ランダムフォーレスト (RandomForest) 54
3.2 エキストラツリー (ExtraTree) 55
3.3 エキストラツリーズ (ExtraTrees) 56
3.4 グラディエントブースティング (GradientBoosting) .. 57
3.5 バッギング (Bagging) 58
3.6 多数決分類器 (VotingClassifier) 60

第 4 章　アンサンブル機械学習の応用事例　　63

 4.0　クレジットカードのデフォルトの学習 . . . .　63

 4.1　赤ワインの品質を判別できる人工ソムリエ . . . .　67

第 5 章　OpenCV と畳み込みニューラルネットワーク　81

 5.0　OpenCV と人工知能 . . . .　85

 5.1　畳み込みニューラルネットワークで絵画を生成 . . . .　93

付　録　　111
索　引　　113

第0章
機械学習の基礎と環境設定

この章では,機械学習の基礎と,本書で紹介するプログラムを実行するためのWindowsパソコンの実行環境設定を説明します.

0.0 機械学習とは

図0.0に示すように,機械学習とは,入力(x)と出力(y)の入出力関数$y = f(x)$を学習することです.すなわち,機械学習では,学習器にデータ(入力と出力)を与えることで,関数$f(x)$を決定していきます.xが未知の入力であれば,学習された関数fに未知の入力を代入すると,f(未知の入力:x)は予測値を生成できます.

図0.0に示すブラックボックスは機械学習器あるいは分類器と呼ばれ,その学習器は,アルゴリズムによって変わります.機械学習器に入力データ(x)

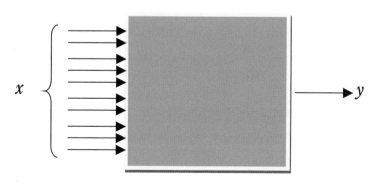

図 0.0 機械学習の概念図 $y = f(x)$

を与えることによって，関数 $f(x)$ は学習しながら複雑な変化をします．最終的に，関数 $f(x)$ は正しい出力 (y) あるいは正しい出力に近い値を生成できるようになります．

　従来の統計学では，人間が重回帰式を考案・構築し（モデル構築），重回帰式の係数（パラメータ）を求めるのがデータ分析の手法でした．

　本書で説明する機械学習では，我々が重回帰式を与えることなく，データを学習器に与えることによって自動的にモデル構築し，入出力関数 $f(x)$ を決定します．機械学習によって構築された入出力関数 $f(x)$ は重回帰式のような単純な構造ではなく，たいへん複雑な構造を持った関数になります．

---
keywords

ブラックボックス，入出力関数 $y = f(x)$，機械学習器，学習器，分類器，モデル構築

0.1　機械学習実行環境設定

　本書では，64 ビット OS の Windows 10 パソコンにおける実行環境構築を中心に説明していきます．Windows 7 や Windows 8.1 でも，環境構築は同様です．パソコンが 64 ビットか 32 ビットかを調べるには，Windows 10 の Cortana に"システム情報"と入力してください．"システムの種類"に 32 か 64 が表示されます．

　システムインストールにはリスクが伴うので，必ず重要な書類はバックアップを取ってから環境構築をしていきましょう．

　ここで説明する実行環境は，3つあります．1つは，Windows OS 上で，機械学習を直接実行できる環境構築です．実行スピードは速いのですが，インストールに手間がかかります．

　2つ目の実行環境は，Windows OS に VMware-workstation-player を実装してから，VMware 上に Linux OS を構築し，Linux 上で機械学習を実行します．実行スピードは遅くなりますが，インストールは極めて簡単です．

　1つ目のほうが当然，実行スピードは格段に速いのですが，実行環境を構築する手間が多くかかるので，2つ目の方法をお勧めします．

　著者の推薦としては，最初に2つ目の方法を構築して，自信がついてから，1つ目の機械学習環境を Windows 上に構築したほうがよいと思います．ま

た，両方の環境を同時に構築しても，まったく問題は生じません．

　3つ目の方法は，64ビットWindows 10のみで可能です．実は，簡単に機械学習環境を構築できますが，インターネット上に情報が極めて少ないので，困った時の解決方法が見つけにくいという難点があります．Windows 10上に"Windows 10 Anniversary Update"をインストールすることで，UbuntuをWindows上にインストールできます．UbuntuとWindowsが同時に動作する環境になります．

- **keywords**
Windows 10，VMware-workstation-player，Linux，Ubuntu，Windows 10 Anniversary Update，64ビットOS

0.1.0 Windows上で直接実行できる環境構築

　下記の方法に従って，実行環境を構築していきます．Python, Cygwin, pip, scipy, numpy, scikit-learnの順にインストールしていきます．

1. Pythonのインストール

　下記サイトから，Python 2.7.12 [1] をWebブラウザ経由でダウンロードします．64ビットOS用では，下記サイトからダウンロードします．
https://www.python.org/ftp/python/2.7.12/**python-2.7.12.amd64.msi**

　ダウンロードしたpython-2.7.12.amd64.msiファイルをダブルクリックしてインストールします．

　Pythonをインストールするフォルダは，**C:¥Python27**にします．

　32ビットOSでは，下記サイトからpython-2.7.12.msiファイルをダウンロードします
https://www.python.org/ftp/python/2.7.12/**python-2.7.12.msi**

　実行するPythonのインストール先のファルダの位置を間違えないようにしましょう．

- **keywords**
Python2.7.12, Cygwin, pip, scipy, numpy, scikit-learn (sklearn)

[1] 本書は，Python 2.7.12での動作確認を行ったうえで執筆しました．後継バージョンでは，操作や結果が異なる場合があります．

2. Cygwin のインストール

Cygwin の terminal から実行できる環境を構築します．Cygwin は，Windows 上に Unix-like な環境を提供します．

2.1 Cygwin ファイルのダウンロードとインストール

下記サイトから，ブラウザ経由で cygwin のインストールファイルをダウンロードし，そのファイルをダブルクリックして Cygwin をインストールします．

https://www.cygwin.com/

64 ビット版のパソコンでは，setup-x86_64.exe ファイルをダウンロードします．

https://www.cygwin.com/**setup-x86_64.exe**

32 ビット版では，setup-x86.exe ファイルをダウンロードします．

https://www.cygwin.com/**setup-x86.exe**

setup-x86_64.exe または setup-x86.exe ファイルをダブルクリックすると，インストール画面が現れます．

1. 最初は，Install from Internet を選択します．
2. Root Directory に次のテキストを入力します．
   C:¥cygwin
3. Local Package Directory にも同じテキストを入力します．
   C:¥cygwin
4. 次に，Direct Connection を選択します．
5. Choose a Download Site では，ftp://ftp.iij.ad.jp を選択します．
6. Select Packages では，次の必要なソフトウエアをインストールします．
   vim Vi IMproved - enhanced vi editor
   nano Enhanced clone of Pico editor
   openssh The OpenSSH server and client
   wget Utility to retrieve files

インストールするには，Skip のアイコンをクリックすればモードが変化し，そのパッケージのバージョン番号が表示されます．「次へ」のボタンをクリッ

クし，選んだパッケージを自動的にインストールします．すべてインストールが終わったら，必ずパソコンを再起動してください．

2.2 Cygwin の環境設定

Cygwin が正しくインストールされていれば，デスクトップの画面にCygwin64Terminal のアイコンが生成されています．そのアイコンをダブルクリックすると，bash 画面が現れます．bash とはターミナル上の shell コマンドです．

`/usr/bin/pwd` と入力してから Enter キーを押してください．directory 名が表示されます．xxx はパソコンのユーザー名になります．私の場合，`/home/takefuji` が表示されます．
`/home/xxx`

nano エディタを用いて次のテキストを入力し，セーブします (control-o, Enter, control-x)．
```
$ nano .bashrc
take='http://web.sfc.keio.ac.jp/~takefuji'
```

`$ echo $take` と入力すると，先ほど入力したテキストが表示されます．
次のコマンドで，アイスクリームのデータをダウンロードしておきます．
```
$ wget $take/ice.csv
```

3. Windows で Python ライブラリをインストール

Windows では，以下のサイトにある binary（実行ファイル）をダウンロードすることで，簡単にインストールできます．

3.1 pip のインストール

get-pip.py ファイルを下記サイトからダウンロードして，pip コマンドをインストールします．

https://bootstrap.pypa.io/**get-pip.py**

Cygwin を立ち上げて，次のように入力します．
```
$ cd /cygdrive/c/users/xxx/Downloads
```

ここで xxx はパソコンのユーザー名です．

Pythonのさまざまなライブラリをインストールするためのpipコマンドをインストールします。

```
$ /cygdrive/c/python27/python get-pip.py
```

Windows 10では，Cortanaに"システム詳細"を入力すると，システムプロパティの画面がPOPされます．環境変数をクリックし，システム環境変数のpathをダブルクリックします．環境変数名の編集の画面がPOPされるので，新規(N)ボタンをクリックし，`C:¥Python27¥Scripts`を入力して，OKボタンを押します．

pipが正しくインストールされたかどうかを確認するために，次のコマンドを実行します．

```
$ which pip
```

/cygdrive/c/python27/Scripts/pip が表示されます．

3.2 パッケージのインストール

Pythonライブラリに必要なパッケージをpipコマンドでインストールします．

Python2.7では，次のVisual C++ 2008パッケージ (vcredist_x64.exe) をインストールしておく必要があります．

http://www.microsoft.com/en-us/download/details.aspx?id=15336

Python3.5では，次のVisual C++ 2015パッケージ (vc_redist.x64.exe) をインストールします．

https://www.microsoft.com/en-us/download/details.aspx?id=48145

多くの重要なPythonライブラリは次のサイトからダウンロードし，以下のコマンドを実行してインストールします．

http://www.lfd.uci.edu/~gohlke/pythonlibs/

xxx.whlファイルをインストールするときは，次のコマンドを実行します．

```
$ pip install xxx.whl
```

最新のpipコマンドをインストールする場合は，upgradeのオプションで実行します．

```
$ pip install --upgrade pip
```

> **keywords**
> get-pip.py, pip install, which, cd, echo, vi, nano, openssh, wget, Visual C++ 2008, Visual C++ 2015

3.3 scikit-learn ライブラリのインストール

scikit-learn ライブラリの解説では，scipy ライブラリが必要です．

次のサイトから scipy ファイル，scipy-0.18.0-cp27-cp27m-win_amd64.whl をダウンロードしてからインストールします．

http://www.lfd.uci.edu/~gohlke/pythonlibs/#scipy

インストールするには，pip コマンドを使います．
```
$ pip install scipy-0.18.0-cp27-cp27m-win_amd64.whl
```

次に，scipy ライブラリと同様に，重要な numpy ライブラリファイルをダウンロードしてインストールします．

http://www.lfd.uci.edu/~gohlke/pythonlibs/#numpy

Python 27 で 64 ビット Windows の場合，上のサイトから次のファイルをダウンロードします．

numpy-1.12.0b1+mkl-cp27-cp27m-win_amd64.whl

ダウンロードしたファイル m-win_amd64.whl を，次のコマンドを実行してインストールします．
```
$ pip install numpy-1.12.0b1+mkl-cp27-cp27m-win_amd64.whl
```

numpy ライブラリの解説では，次のインテルのサイトにおける Intel Math Kernel Library が必要であると記述されていますが，Python 27 では，numpy ライブラリは Microsoft Visual C++ 2008 に依存しているので，Visual C++ 2008 パッケージで十分です．参考のために，方法のみを記述します．

64 ビット OS では，vcredist_x64.exe ファイルを下記サイトからダウンロードして，そのファイルをダブルクリックしてインストールします．

https://www.microsoft.com/en-us/download/details.aspx?id=15336

32 ビット OS では，次のサイトから vcredist_x86.exe をダウンロードします．vcredist_x64.exe ファイルか vcredist_x86.exe ファイルをダブルクリックしてインストールします．また，w_mkl_11.3.3.207.exe ファイルをダウンロードしてインストールする必要があります．

https://software.intel.com/en-us/intel-mkl

w_mkl_11.3.3.207.exe は，500MB ほどある大きなファイルです．

scikit-learn ライブラリの解説では，scipy ライブラリが必要であると書いてあります．次のサイトから scipy ファイル，scipy-0.18.0-cp27-cp27m-win_amd64.whl ファイルをダウンロードし，そのファイルをダブルクリックすることで，ライブラリをインストールできます．

http://www.lfd.uci.edu/~gohlke/pythonlibs/#scipy

numpy のインストールが完了していれば，最も重要な scikit-learn ライブラリをインストールできます．次のサイトから，vcredist_x86.exe ファイルダウンロードし，そのファイルをダブルクリックすることでインストールします．

http://www.lfd.uci.edu/~gohlke/pythonlibs/#scikit-learn

Python 27 で 64 ビット Windows の場合，上のサイトから次のファイルをダウンロードします．

scikit_learn-0.18.1-cp27-cp27m-win_amd64.whl

ダウンロードしたファイルをインストールするには，次のコマンドを実行します．

```
$ pip install scikit_learn-0.18.1-cp27-cp27m-win_amd64.whl
```

すべての xxx.whl ファイルは，pip コマンドで簡単にインストールできます．

```
$ pip install xxx.whl
```

まとめると，Python，Cygwin をインストールしてから，pip コマンドをインストールします．Python 2.7 の場合は，Visual C++ 2008 パッケージをインストールします．Python 3.5 では，Visual C++ 2015 パッケージをインストールします．Windows の path の設定は重要です．scipy，numpy，scikit-learn(sklearn)，その他のライブラリ (xxx.whl) を http://www.lfd.uci.

edu/~gohlke/pythonlibs/からダウンロードし，`$ pip install xxx.whl`コマンドでインストールできます．

0.1.1 Linux 上で実行できる環境構築

Linux 実行環境を構築するために，VMware Workstation Player をパソコンにインストールします．VMware に Ubuntu 14.04.5 をインストールしてから，Ubuntu の terminal を起動して，Python ライブラリ (scipy, numpy, scikit-learn) をインストールします．

(1) VMware Workstation Player をネットで検索し，70MB ほどのファイルをダウンロードし，ダブルクリックしてインストールします．
(2) ubuntu 14.04.5 desktop site:jp でネット検索します．ubuntu-14.04.5-desktop-amd64.iso ファイル (1G) をダウンロードします．
(3) VMware を起動し，新規仮想マシンの作成をクリックします．先ほどダウンロードした iso ファイルをインストーラディスクイメージファイルで参照して設定します．フルネーム，ユーザー名，パスワードを設定し，仮想マシン名，場所を設定します．ディスクの容量は，20GB あれば十分です．
(4) 作成した仮想マシンの再生ボタンをクリックします．インストールが開始し，終了すると login 画面が現れます．ユーザー名とパスワードを入力し，Ubuntu システムに login します．
(5) Ubuntu Desktop の左側の一番トップのアイコンをクリックすると，サーチ画面が表示されます．ここで，`terminal` と入力し，画面に表示された terminal をクリックします．左に terminal アイコンが現れるので，右クリックし，Lock to Launcher を設定します．左のアイコンを 1 クリックするだけで terminal が起動できるようになります．
(6) `sudo su` と入力するとスーパーユーザーになります．スーパーユーザーになると，プロンプトが `$` マークから `#` マークに変わります．
```
# apt update
# apt upgrade
```
VMware の右上ボタンをクリックし，パワーオフします．
(7) VMware tools をインストールします．VMware 画面の左上に Player(P) をクリックし，管理 (M) メニューを開き VMware Tools を選択します．ここで，次のコマンドを実行してください．

$ df

$ cd /media/ を入力しTabキーを押しながら，ユーザー名が出てきたら，その最初の文字を入れてからTabキーを押せば，自動的にユーザー名が入力されます．さらに，Tabキーを押してからEnterキーを押します．

$ pwd

/media/xxx/VMware Tools と表示されます．ここで，xxxはユーザー名です．

$ cp VMwareTools-yyy.tar.gz ~/ yyyはバージョン番号です．これもTabキーを使って自動入力させます．

$ cd

$ tar xvf VWwareTools

Tabキーを押して，Enterキーを押します．

$ cd vmware-tools-distrib

$ sudo ./vmware-install.pl

$ df

/mnt/hgfs が画面に表示されたら，共有フォルダの設定が可能になります．

(8) 共有フォルダの設定

パソコンのデスクトップにフォルダを作成します．フォルダの名前は，ubuntu にします．

VMware の Player(P) →管理 (M) →仮想マシン設定を起動します．オプションメニューの共有フォルダを常に有効にします．フォルダの追加ボタンをクリックして，ホストフォルダのubuntuフォルダを選ぶと，名前とホストパスが次のように表示されます．xxxはパソコンのユーザー名です．ユーザー名はなるべく英語にしましょう．

名前	ホストパス
ubuntu	C:¥Users¥xxx¥Desktop¥ubuntu

$ cd /mnt/ を入力しTabキーを2回押し，Enterキーを押します．

$ cd /mnt/hgfs/ubuntu

$ echo 'Hi' >help.txt

ここで，パソコンからhelp.txtファイルを開いてください．"Hi"のテキストが確認できれば，VMware上の/mnt/hgfs/ubuntuフォルダと，パソコンのubuntuフォルダは共有されていることが確認できます．

(9) Python ライブラリのインストール

Linux では，極めて簡単に必要な Python ライブラリがインストールできます．
```
$ sudo apt install python-pandas
$ sudo apt install python-sklearn
```

nano エディタを用いて，次のテキストを入力し，セーブします (control-o, Enter, control-x).
```
$ nano .bashrc
take='http://web.sfc.keio.ac.jp/~takefuji'
```
　$ echo $take と入力すると，先ほど入力したテキストが表示されます．次のコマンドで，アイスクリームのデータをダウンロードしておきます．
```
$ wget $take/ice.csv
```

---
keywords
PATH, sudo, apt update, apt upgrade, df, pwd, tar

0.1.2　Ubuntu を Windows 10 上で直接動作させる

Microsoft 社は，Windows 10 から Ubuntu 環境を提供するようになりました．"Windows 10 Anniversary Update" をインストールすると，意外と簡単に Ubuntu をインストールできます．したがって，VMware をインストールする必要もありませんし，実行スピードも飛躍的に向上しました．Windows 10 Anniversary Update をインストールするためには，下記の方法を試してください．

(1) Cortana で，update と入力すると更新の画面が現れます．
　"詳細情報" をクリックすると，"Windows 10 Anniversary Update 入手" の画面が現れるのでクリックし，ダウンロードしてインストールします．
　あるいは，"Anniversary Update" 入手のキーワードでネット検索すると，microsoft.com のサイトが直接現れます．
(2) Cortana で developer と入力すると，開発者向け設定画面が現れるので，開発者モードを選択します．
(3) Cortana に，windows features と入力すると，Windows の機能の有効

化または無効化の画面が現れます．

(4) Windows の機能の有効化画面で，SMB1.0/CFS, Windows PowerShell2.0, Windows Subsystem for Linux(Beta) の 3 つのボタンを ON にします（図 0.1）．

図 **0.1** Windows 10 に Ubuntu をインストール

(5) Windows を再起動します．
(6) Cortana に `bash` と入力すると，Bash on Ubuntu on Windows と表示されるので，そのアイコンをクリックします．
(7) bash の画面が表示されたら，y と入力すれば，ファイルのダウンロードが始まり，Ubuntu のインストールが始まります．しばらくするとインストールは自動的に完了します．
(8) もう一度，Cortana に `bash` と入力して，クリックすると bash 画面が現れます．
(9) bash の画面で，`lsb_release -a` と入力してみましょう．Ubuntu のバージョン情報を表示します．

　`$ sudo su` と入力すればスーパーユーザーになります．パスワードを要求される場合は，パソコンのパスワードを入力してください．

　後は，必要なライブラリを下記コマンドでインストールするだけです．スーパーユーザーになるとプロンプトが `$` マークから `#` マークに変わります．

次に，pip コマンドをインストールします．
```
# apt install python-pip
```

pip コマンドを upgrade します．
```
# pip install --upgrade pip
```

python-pandas ライブラリをインストールします．
```
# apt install python-pandas
```

機械学習のライブラリ (python-sklearn) をインストールします．
```
# apt install python-sklearn
```

次のコマンドで，システムを update, upgrade します．
```
# apt update
# apt upgrade
```

nano エディタを用いて，次のテキストを入力し，セーブします (control-o, Enter, control-x)．
```
$ nano .bashrc
take='http://web.sfc.keio.ac.jp/~takefuji'
```

$ echo $take と入力すると，先ほど入力したテキストが表示されます．
次のコマンドで，アイスクリームのデータをダウンロードしておきます．
```
$ wget $take/ice.csv
```

一般に，ライブラリ xxx は次のコマンドでインストールします．
```
# apt install xxx
```

また，最新のライブラリ xxx を pip コマンドでインストールできます．
```
# pip install --upgrade xxx
```

ライブラリの名前が分からない場合は，次のコマンドでライブラリ名を表示できます．
```
# apt search xxx
```

```
# pip search xxx
```

インストールしたライブラリをuninstallするには，次のコマンドを実行します．

```
# apt-get purge xxx
# pip uninstall xxx
```

古くて必要のないライブラリを自動的に削除するには，次のコマンドを実行します．

```
# apt-get autoremove
```

インストールしたライブラリの矛盾を正すには，次のコマンドを実行します．

```
# apt-get install -f
```

xxxライブラリがインストールされているかどうか確認するには，次のコマンドを実行します．

```
# dpkg -l | grep xxx
# pip list | grep xxx
```

---
keywords

Cortana, dpkg, apt install, apt search, pip uninstall, apt-get autoremove, apt-get purge, pip list, pip search, apt-get install -f

---

第1章

ビッグデータ解析と機械学習

1.0 ビッグデータ解析とは

　英語の Wikipedia の解説によれば，ビッグデータとは，市販されているデータベース管理ツールや従来のデータ処理アプリケーションで処理することが困難なほど**巨大または複雑な**データ集合の集積物を表す用語のことです．日本語の Wikipedia の解説は誤訳で，"**巨大で複雑な**" となっていますが，英語の Wikipedia では，so large or complex になっています．つまり，単にデータの大きさを議論しているのではなく，複雑なデータの関係を分析・解析することを意味します．本書の目的は，機械学習技術を使ってビッグデータ解析することです．

　本書で説明する機械学習手法を使うと，従来の統計手法・分析手法ではできなかった "正確な予測"，"データモデル構築の自動化"，"データの自動特徴分析" の3つを実現できます．現在の最先端機械学習手法は，最新の統計手法を組み入れ，既知のビッグデータから正確な予測ができるようになりました．

　本章では，最初に，最小二乗法 OLS，一般化最小二乗法 GLS，加重最小二乗法 WLS，ロバスト線形モデル RLM，Lasso 線形モデル，自己相関付き実行可能一般化最小二乗法 GLSAR，混合線形モデル MixedLM，分位点回帰 QuantReg，OMP 手法，イラスティックネット ElasticNet などを説明します．

　機械学習手法では，サポートベクトル回帰 SVR，カーネルリッジ回帰 KRR，ガウジアン・ナイーブ・ベイズ GaussianNB，決定木分類器 DecisionTreeClassifier，3つの近傍法 (KNeighborsRegressor, KNeighborsClassifier, RadiusNeighborsClassifier)，確率的勾配降下法 SGDClassifier，ディープラーニング

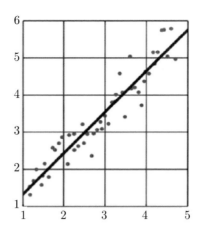

図 1.0　単回帰式 ($y = ax + c$)：データから a と c を計算する

ニューラルネットワーク keras を紹介します．

1.1　重回帰分析とは

　重回帰分析を説明する前に，最初に単回帰分析を説明します．単回帰分析では，1つの目的変数 (y) を1つの説明変数 (x) で予測するもので，その2変量の間の関係性を y (縦軸)，x (横軸)，定数 (a, c) を使って単回帰式で表現します．簡単に説明すると，入力 (x) と出力 (y) の次式の関係式において，係数 (a, c) を求めることになります．

$$y = ax + c$$

　図 1.0 では，プロットされた点がデータを表しています．プロットされたデータから傾き (a) と定数 (c) を計算することが単回帰分析になります．
　重回帰分析では，2つ以上の説明変数が必要です．本書では，最高気温と通行人数の2つの説明変数に，アイスクリームの売上げ額の目的変数のデータを使います．
　下記サイトには，最高気温，通行人数，アイスクリームの売上げデータがあります．
http://web.sfc.keio.ac.jp/~takefuji/ice.csv
　ice.csv データファイルをダウンロードしてから，重回帰分析を行っていき

ます．データファイルをダウンロードするには，Cygwin ターミナルあるいは Ubuntu ターミナルから次のコマンドを実行します．$take が利用できるように，.bashrc ファイルに take='http://web.sfc.keio.ac.jp/~takefuji' を入力しておきましょう．テキストファイルに入力するには，nano エディタか vi を使います．

$ wget $take/ice.csv

あるいは，

$ wget http://web.sfc.keio.ac.jp/~takefuji/ice.csv

アイスクリーム売上げの重回帰式は次のようになります：説明変数 ($x1, x2$)，目的変数 (y)，定数 (c)，temp と street は求めたい重回帰式の係数になります．$X = (x1, x2)$ とすると，説明変数は X となります．重回帰分析の目的は，temp と street の係数を求めることです．

$$y = \text{temp} * x1 + \text{street} * x2 + c$$

従来の統計手法では，R-squared 値（実際のデータと予測値のフィット度）が予測の正確さを表現します．R-squared 値が 1 に近いほど予測が正確であることを意味します．また，R-squared 値が 0 に近いほど予測が悪いことを示しています．

読者諸氏は想像できると思いますが，説明変数がたくさんある場合は，どのような重回帰式を考案するかが難しい問題となります．重回帰式の良しあしで，分析結果が左右されます．本書で説明する機械学習では，この重回帰式の問題を解決し，重回帰式を考える必要がありません．機械学習とは，データ（入力と出力）を学習器に与えることで，自動的にモデルを作成し，データを予測できる画期的な方法です．

―― keywords ――――――――――――――――――――――――
R-squared, 説明変数, 目的変数, 定数

1.1.0　最小二乗法 OLS

ここでは，statsmodels の Python ライブラリを使います．最小二乗法 OLS (Ordinary Least Square) のアルゴリズムを使ったプログラム (ols.py) は非常に短く，たったの 8 行です．

ols.py
```
import pandas as pd
import statsmodels.api as sm
data=pd.read_csv('ice.csv')
x=data[['temp','street']]
x=sm.add_constant(x)
y=data['ice']
est=sm.OLS(y,x).fit()
print(est.summary())
```

Python のライブラリは，import で呼び出すことができます．1 行目のコマンド，import pandas as pd により pandas を pd と短い別名で指定できます．alias 機能と呼ばれています．ice.csv ファイルは次のようなデータです．

```
$ cat ice.csv
date,ice,temp,street
2012/8/1,12220,26,4540
2012/8/2,15330,32,5250
2012/8/3,11680,32,6000
2012/8/4,12640,29,5120
2012/8/5,15150,34,4640
2012/8/6,16440,33,8620
2012/8/7,16080,35,5810
2012/8/8,9830,34,4170
2012/8/9,14520,29,5160
2012/8/10,14610,34,4260
2012/8/11,11570,28,4910
2012/8/12,11290,34,5870
2012/8/13,10770,26,5580
2012/8/14,13890,30,5660
2012/8/15,12060,30,4330
2012/8/16,18830,34,6410
2012/8/17,12160,25,4130
2012/8/18,6550,30,4390
2012/8/19,9420,31,5650
```

2012/8/20,10480,26,5150
2012/8/21,13610,27,5560
2012/8/22,17380,29,7540
2012/8/23,18540,29,8920
2012/8/24,13090,30,7830
2012/8/25,12990,30,4050
2012/8/26,15070,35,5040
2012/8/27,10020,30,4050
2012/8/28,16070,30,5200
2012/8/29,16540,31,8810
2012/8/30,20030,26,8870
2012/8/31,11160,27,4410

2行目のコマンドは，`import statsmodels.api as sm`，つまり statsmodels.api ライブラリを利用する宣言をしています．ここでも，alias 機能を使い，statsmodels.api ライブラリを sm と定義しました．

import コマンドを使うと，簡単に，自作のプログラムの中で複雑なライブラリを利用できます．

3行目のコマンド，`data=pd.read_csv('ice.csv')`，すなわち読み込まれたデータは data 変数に格納します．pandas コマンド (`pd.read_csv`) で，csv ファイル（カンマで区切られたデータ）を簡単に読み取り，コラム属性データを自由自在に切り出すことができます．data ファイル (ice.csv) の1行目のコラム属性で，列方向のデータを簡単に切り出すことができます．data ファイルの1行目には，date,ice,temp,street の4つのコラム属性があります．

例えば，プログラム6行目，`y=data['ice']` の場合，アイスクリームの売上データ（1列）のみが変数 y に代入されます．

pandas コマンドで複数のコラム属性を切り出すことができます．例えば，2つのコラム属性 (temp, street) を切り出したい場合，4行目の `x=data[['temp','street']]` のように，temp のデータと street のデータの2列分のデータを切り出し，その2列のデータを変数 x に代入します．

プログラム5行目の `x=sm.add_constant(x)` は，重回帰式の定数を設定しています．

一番重要なコマンドは，プログラム7行目の `est=sm.OLS(y,x).fit()` です．statsmodels ライブラリの OLS アルゴリズム（最小二乗法）を使って，fit() 関

数で最小二乗フィッティングを実行させます．`est=sm.OLS(y,x).fit()` で，計算結果が変数 est に代入されます．

プログラムの最終行，8 行目，`print(est.summary())` は，計算結果を表示します．

ols.py プログラムファイルをダウンロードしてから，"`python ols.py`" コマンドを実行すると，OLS アルゴリズムの重回帰分析の実行結果を表示します．ols.py ファイルのダウンロードには，"`wget $take/ols.py`" コマンドを実行します．エラーが出た場合は，nano か vi エディタを用いて，下記の 1 行を.bashrc ファイルに必ず付加してください．
`take='http://web.sfc.keio.ac.jp/~takefuji'`

計算結果の中で，特に重視しなくてはいけないパラメータは，R-squared と coef の値です．次のコマンドを実行していきます（.bashrc ファイルの変更を source コマンドで OS に認識させます）．
```
$ source .bashrc
```

ice.csv ファイルをダウンロードします．
```
$ wget $take/ice.csv
```

ols.py をダウンロードします．
```
$ wget $take/ols.py
```

ols.py ファイルを Python で実行します．
```
$ python ols.py
```

ここでエラーが出る場合は，pandas ライブラリがうまくインストールされていないのかもしれません．

Windows であれば，次のコマンドを実行します．
```
$ pip install --upgrade pandas
```

Ubuntu であれば，次のコマンドを実行します
```
$ sudo pip install --upgrade pandas
```

pandas ライブラリのインストールでエラーが出なければ，もう一度, python

ols.py を実行してください．

R-squared: 0.450

係数名	coef
const	794.1355
temp	176.1438
street	1.3104

重回帰式: $y = \text{temp} * x1 + \text{street} * x2 + c$

つまり，重回帰式では，定数 $c = 794$，temp $= 176$，street $= 1.31$ となります．R-squared 値は重回帰式の決定係数（フィット係数）のことで，1.0 はパーフェクト，0.0 はまったくフィットしていないと解釈できます．この場合は，R-squared $= 0.45$ なので，フィット係数はそれほど良くありません．

─ **pandas ライブラリを試してみる** ─

先ほどの ols.py を変更して，pandas ライブラリの機能を試すために，次の 2 行を加えてみます．

```
x=data[['temp']]
print(x)
```

test.py を見ると，temp だけを切り出してきて，表示してくれます．pandas ライブラリは，ビッグデータ解析で重要な機能，データコラムの切り出しを簡単なコマンドで実行してくれます．

test.py
```
import pandas as pd
data=pd.read_csv('ice.csv')
x=data[['temp']]
print(x)}
```

```
$ python test.py
temp
0 26
1 32
2 32
  ⋮
```

```
29  26
30  27
```

実際のアイスクリームの売上げと，予測した売上げをグラフ表示して，直感的に決定係数（フィット係数）を表示してくれるプログラム（olsGUI.py）を次に示します．olsGUI.py のプログラムでは，先ほどの ols.py にグラフ表示機能を付加しただけです．

olsGUI.py
```
from math import *
import pandas as pd
import numpy as np
import statsmodels.api as sm
import matplotlib.pyplot as plt
data=pd.read_csv('ice.csv')
x=data[['temp','street']]
x=sm.add_constant(x)
y=data['ice']
est=sm.OLS(y,x).fit()
print(est.summary())
t=np.arange(0.0,31.0)
e=est.predict(x)
plt.plot(t,y,'-b')
plt.plot(t,e,'--b')
plt.legend(('real','OLS'))
plt.show()
```

グラフ表示では，matplotlib ライブラリを使います．プログラムの5行目，import matplotlib.pyplot as plt は，matplotlib ライブラリを plt として利用します．

グラフの横軸は，プログラム中の t=np.arange(0.0,31.0) によって，0.0 から 30 の 31 個を表示します．

グラフの縦軸では，2本線を表示します．プログラム中の plt.plot(t,y,'-b') は実データを表示，plt.plot(t,e,'--b') は予測データを表示します．plt.plot() 関数には，横軸 (t)，縦軸 (y)，グラフ線の種類 ('--b') を指定します．

グラフに表示する線の種類では，'--' は大きい破線，':' は細かい破線，

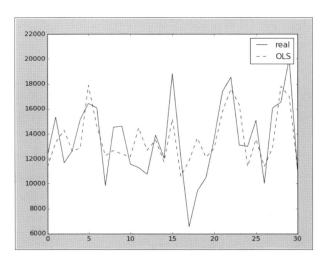

図 1.1 OLS アルゴリズムの結果（破線は OLS による予測，実線は実際の売上げ）

'-' は実線，'-.' は 1 点鎖線を指定できます．

　グラフ線の色の指定は，b は青，r は赤，g は緑，c はシアン，m はマゼンタ，y は黄，k は黒，w は白になります．

　プログラム中の `plt.legend(('real','OLS'))` では，legend 関数は凡例を表示します．プログラム中の `plt.show()` によって，グラフ表示機能を起動します．

---- 表示線のまとめ ----
'--' は大きい破線，':' は細かい破線，'-' は実線，'-.' は 1 点鎖線

---- 表示線の色 ----
b はブルー，r は赤，g は緑，c はシアン，m はマゼンタ，y は黄，k は黒，w は白

`$ wget $take/olsGUI.py` で olsGUI.py をダウンロードし，`$ python olsGUI.py` のコマンドを実行すると，図 1.1 に示す結果を表示します．

---- keywords ----
pandas, import, fit() 関数, source, matplotlib, plt.plot, グラフ線の種類, グラフ線の色

1.1.1　一般化最小二乗法 GLS

　一般化最小二乗法 GLS (Generalized Least Squares) と最小二乗法 (OLS) のアルゴリズムとの違いは，7 行目だけです．est=sm.GLS(y,x).fit() を実行するだけで，一般化最小二乗法 GLS アルゴリズムの予測をします．このように，アルゴリズムを変えても，プログラム全体の構造は変わりません．つまり，苦労することなく簡単にいろいろなアルゴリズムを試すことができます．

gls.py
```
import pandas as pd
import statsmodels.api as sm
data=pd.read_csv('ice.csv')
x=data[['temp','street']]
x=sm.add_constant(x)
y=data['ice']
est=sm.GLS(y,x).fit()
print(est.summary())
```

　`$ wget $take/gls.py` で gls.py をダウンロードし，`$ python gls.py` のコマンドを実行します．実行結果は，OLS と同じでした．

R-squared: 0.450

係数名	coef
const	794.1355
temp	176.1438
street	1.3104

1.1.2　加重最小二乗法 WLS

　wls.py は加重最小二乗法 WLS (Weighted Least Squares) のプログラムです．7 行目のコマンド，est=sm.WLS(y,x).fit() で，加重最小二乗法 WLS アルゴリズムを実行します．

```
wls.py
import pandas as pd
import statsmodels.api as sm
data=pd.read_csv('ice.csv')
x=data[['temp','street']]
x=sm.add_constant(x)
y=data['ice']
est=sm.WLS(y,x).fit()
print est.summary()
```

`$ wget $take/wls.py` で wls.py をダウンロードし，`$ python wls.py` のコマンドを実行します．この実行結果も，OLS や GLS とまったく同じでした．

R-squared: 0.450

係数名	coef
const	794.1355
temp	176.1438
street	1.3104

1.1.3 ロバスト線形モデル RLM

ロバスト線形モデル RLM (Robust Linear Model) の中には，6 つの評価基準関数が実装されています．6 つの評価基準関数とは，HuberT，LeastSquares，AndrewWave，RamsayE，TrimmedMean，Hampel です．

残念ながら，ロバスト線形モデル RLM には，R-squared 値を計算する関数が用意されていません．そこで，sklearn.metrics ライブラリの r2_score 関数を利用して，R-squared 値を計算します．リアル値と予測値を，r2_score (リアル値,予測値) 関数に代入するだけで，簡単に R-squared 値が計算できます．

例えば，`r2=r2_score(y,est1.predict(x))` コマンドを実行すると，変数 r2 に R-squared 値が代入されます．

```
rlm.py
import pandas as pd
import statsmodels.api as sm
from sklearn.metrics import r2_score
```

```
data=pd.read_csv('ice.csv')
x=data[['temp','street']]
x=sm.add_constant(x)
y=data['ice']
est1=sm.RLM(y,x,M=sm.robust.norms.HuberT()).fit()
est2=sm.RLM(y,x,M=sm.robust.norms.LeastSquares()).fit()
est3=sm.RLM(y,x,M=sm.robust.norms.AndrewWave()).fit()
est4=sm.RLM(y,x,M=sm.robust.norms.RamsayE()).fit()
est5=sm.RLM(y,x,M=sm.robust.norms.TrimmedMean ()).fit()
est6=sm.RLM(y,x,M=sm.robust.norms.Hampel()).fit()
r2=r2_score(y,est1.predict(x))
print('R-squared:',r2)
print(est1.summary2())
r2=r2_score(y,est2.predict(x))
print('R-squared:',r2)
print(est2.summary2())
r2=r2_score(y,est3.predict(x))
print('R-squared:',r2)
print(est3.summary2())
r2=r2_score(y,est4.predict(x))
print('R-squared:',r2)
print(est4.summary2())
r2=r2_score(y,est5.predict(x))
print('R-squared:',r2)
print(est5.summary2())
r2=r2_score(y,est6.predict(x))
print('R-squared:',r2)
print(est6.summary2())
```

　$ wget $take/rlm.py で rlm.py をダウンロードし，$ python rlm.py のコマンドを実行した結果を，次にまとめて表示します．評価基準関数が変わっても，R-squared 値は 0.45 付近でした．

評価基準関数	R-squared
HuberT	0.4483
LeastSquares	0.450
AndrewWave	0.44826
RamsayE	0.44786
TrimmedMean	0.4439
Hampel	0.450

1.1.4 Lasso 線形モデル

Lasso 線形モデルには，実行結果の summary() 関数がありません．R-squared 値は clf.score(x,y) で計算できます．clf.intercept_関数で，重回帰式の定数の値を表示します．また，clf.coef_関数は，2 つの係数（temp と street）の値を示します．

Lasso 線形モデル clf は，次式で表現します．
`clf=linear_model.Lasso()`

```
lasso.py
import pandas as pd
import numpy as np
import statsmodels.api as sm
from sklearn import linear_model
data=pd.read_csv('ice.csv')
x=data[['temp','street']]
x=sm.add_constant(x)
y=data['ice']
clf=linear_model.Lasso()
clf.fit(x,y)
p=clf.predict(x)
print(clf.score(x,y))
print(clf.intercept_)
print(clf.coef_)
```

$ wget $take/lasso.py で lasso.py をダウンロードし，$ python lasso.py で実行した結果は以下の表のとおりです．

R-squared: 0.450

係数名	coef
const	797.692
temp	176.026
street	1.310

1.1.5　自己相関付き実行可能一般化最小二乗法 GLSAR

名前の長いアルゴリズムですが，GLSAR のアルゴリズムを呼び出して，簡単に演算できます．

自己相関付き実行可能一般化最小二乗法 GLSAR (feasible generalized least squares with autocorrelated AR) モデルは，次式で表現できます．est=sm.GLSAR(y,x).fit()

```
glsar.py
import pandas as pd
import numpy as np
import statsmodels.api as sm
import matplotlib.pyplot as plt
data=pd.read_csv('ice.csv')
x=data[['temp','street']]
x=sm.add_constant(x)
y=data['ice']
est=sm.GLSAR(y,x).fit()
print(est.summary())
```

`$ wget $take/glsar.py` で glsar.py をダウンロードし，`$ python glsar.py` で実行した結果を次の表に示します．

R-squared: 0.450

係数名	coef
const	180.1840
temp	192.3124
street	1.3267

1.1.6 混合線形モデル MixedLM

混合線形モデル MixedLM (Mixed Linear Model) では，predict 関数が（2016 年 12 月時点で）実装されていません．したがって，predict 関数に相当する予測値を計算する工夫が必要になります．

混合線形モデル MixedLM を実行すると，est.params.temp 変数に temp の係数が代入されます．また，同様に，est.params.street 変数に street の係数が代入されます．

重回帰式 (y = temp∗x1+street∗x2+c) の x1 は，x1 = data['temp']，x2 は，x2 = data['street'] でそれぞれ与えられます．c は，c = est.params.Intercept で計算できます．したがって，予測値を求める計算式は次のようになります．

e=est.params.temp*data['temp']
  +est.params.street*data['street']
  +est.params.Intercept

この e 変数は，predict(x) に相当する予測値になります．

混合線形モデルは，次式で表します．

est=sm.MixedLM.from_formula("ice ~ temp + street",data,groups=y).fit()

lmem.py
```
import pandas as pd
import numpy as np
import statsmodels.api as sm
from sklearn.metrics import r2_score
data=pd.read_csv('ice.csv')
x=data[['temp','street']]
x=sm.add_constant(x)
y=data['ice']
est=sm.MixedLM.from_formula("ice ~ temp + street",data,groups=y).
   fit()
print(est.params)
e=est.params.temp*data['temp']+est.params.street*data['street']+
   est.params.Intercept
print('R-squared:',r2_score(y,e))
```

$ wget $take/lmem.py で lmem.py をダウンロードし，$ python lmem.py を実行すると，次のような結果が表示されます．

R-squared: 0.45008111876126478

係数名	coef
Intercept	794.135485
temp	176.143803
street	1.310358

1.1.7　分位点回帰 QuantReg

　分位点回帰 QuantReg (Quantile Regression) のアルゴリズムは，quantreg.py で計算できます．4 行目の quantile_regression 関数が重要な役目を果たします．

　分位点回帰モデルは，次式で表現します．
est=QuantReg(y,x).fit(q=0.99999)

```
quantreg.py

import pandas as pd
import numpy as np
import statsmodels.api as sm
from statsmodels.regression.quantile_regression import QuantReg
import matplotlib.pyplot as plt
data=pd.read_csv('ice.csv')
x=data[['temp','street']]
x=sm.add_constant(x)
y=data['ice']
est=QuantReg(y,x).fit(q=0.99999)
print(est.summary())
```

　今までのアルゴリズム（最小二乗法 OLS，一般化最小二乗法 GLS，加重最小二乗法 WLS，ロバスト線形モデル RLM，Lasso 線形モデル，自己相関付き実行可能一般化最小二乗法 GLSAR，混合線形モデル MixedLM）と違って，分位点回帰のアルゴリズムは，R-squared 値が 0.5757 と高くなっています．

　$ wget $take/quantreg.py で quantreg.py をダウンロードし，$ python quantreg.py コマンドで実行した結果は次のとおりです．

Pseudo R-squared: 0.5757

係数名	coef
const	8.2150
temp	293.0080
street	1.3984

次のプログラム (quantreg2.py) のように，重回帰式を直接書くこともできます．

`est=smf.quantreg('ice ~ temp + street',data).fit(q=.999)`

```
quantreg2.py
import pandas as pd
import numpy as np
import statsmodels.api as sm
import statsmodels.formula.api as smf
from statsmodels.regression.quantile_regression import QuantReg
import matplotlib.pyplot as plt
data=pd.read_csv('ice.csv')
data=sm.add_constant(data)
x=data[['temp','street']]
y=data['ice']
est=smf.quantreg('ice ~ temp + street',data).fit(q=.999)
print est.summary()
```

$ wget $take/quantreg2.py で quantreg2.py をダウンロードし，$ python quantreg2.py を実行した結果を次に表示します．

Pseudo R-squared: 0.5756

係数名	coef
Intercept	706.0653
temp	273.4426
street	1.3770

1.1.8　OMP 手法

OMP 手法 (Orthogonal Matching Pursuit) は，$ python omp.py を実行して演算できます．OMP 法のライブラリ名は，OrthogonalMatchingPursuit

です．

OMP 手法モデルは，次式で表します．
`lm=OrthogonalMatchingPursuit(n_nonzero_coefs=3)`

```
omp.py
import pandas as pd
import numpy as np
import statsmodels.api as sm
from sklearn.linear_model import OrthogonalMatchingPursuit
data=pd.read_csv('ice.csv')
x=data[['temp','street']]
x=sm.add_constant(x)
y=data['ice']
lm=OrthogonalMatchingPursuit(n_nonzero_coefs=3)
est=lm.fit(x,y)
print(est.coef_)
print(est.intercept_)
print(est.score(x,y))
```

`$ wget $take/omp.py` で omp.py をダウンロードし，`$ python omp.py` コマンドで実行した結果は次のようになります．

R-squared: 0.450

係数名	coef
const	794.135
temp	176.14380
street	1.310

1.1.9　イラスティックネット ElasticNet

イラスティックネット ElasticNet (Elastic-net machine learning) は線形モデルに分類されます．このモデルは，次式で表現します．
`clf=ElasticNet(alpha=0.01)`

elasticnet.py

```
import pandas as pd
from sklearn.linear_model import ElasticNet
data=pd.read_csv('ice.csv')
x=data[['temp','street']]
y=data['ice']
clf=ElasticNet(alpha=0.01)
clf.fit(x,y)
print(clf.score(x,y))
```

`$ wget $take/elasticnet.py` で elasticnet.py をダウンロード，`$ python elasticnet.py` コマンドで実行して得られる R-squared 値は 0.450 で，それほど高くはありません．

本章で紹介したさまざまな重回帰分析アルゴリズムの性能比較をまとめてみました．アルゴリズムとその R-squared 値を表 1.0 に示します．

表 1.0 重回帰分析アルゴリズムの R-squared 値の比較

アルゴリズム	R-squared
OLS	0.45
GLS	0.45
WLS	0.45
RLM with HuberT	0.4483
RLM with LeastSquares	0.45
RLM with AndrewWave	0.44826
RLM with RamseyE	0.44786
RLM with TrimmedMean	0.4439
RLM with Hampel	0.45
Lasso	.45
GLSAR	0.45
MixedLM	0.45
QuantReg	0.5757
OMP	0.45
ElasticNet	0.45

第2章

機械学習

　本章では，7種類の機械学習のアルゴリズムを紹介します．各アルゴリズムを以下に列記します．

1. サポートベクトル回帰 SVR
2. カーネルリッジ回帰 KRR
3. ナイーブ・ベイズ（GaussianNB, MultinomialNB, BernoulliNB）
4. 決定木分類器 DecisionTreeClassifier
5. 3つの近傍法 (KNeighborsRegressor, KNeighborsClassifier RadiusNeighborsClassifier)
6. 確率的勾配降下法 SGDClassifier
7. ディープラーニングニューラルネットワーク keras

　何度も繰り返しますが，従来の統計手法と違うのは，我々が重回帰モデルを提供する必要がない点です．ここで説明する機械学習手法では，データを与えることで，入出力関数モデルを自動的に構築します．重回帰式の係数は生成できませんが，重回帰式よりも複雑な入出力関数を生成します．

　つまり，入出力関数は自動的に生成され，従来の重回帰式に比べて，R-squared値が著しく向上します．また，予測値は，clf.predict(x) 関数によって生成できます．ここで，clf は機械学習モデルであり，先ほど述べた機械学習のアルゴリズムで定義できます．

　一般に，機械学習モデル clf は，次のように定義します．ここで，XXX() は機械学習のアルゴリズムです．括弧の中に，さまざまなパラメータを加えることもあります．

　clf=XXX()

2.0 サポートベクトル回帰 SVR

サポートベクトル回帰 SVR (Support Vector Regression) では，SVR 学習器のパラメータ設定が極めて重要です．本書では，次のパラメータの設定で，R-squared 値=0.969 を達成しました．アルゴリズムのライブラリは，SVR です．SVR アルゴリズムには，複数のパラメータが用意され，設定できるようになっています．ここで一番重要なパラメータは C の値です．C はペナルティパラメータです．

サポートベクトル回帰の機械学習モデル clf は，次の式で表します．

clf=SVR(C=1e7,epsilon=.01,max_iter=-1,tol=1e-7,verbose=1,gamma=10.1)

サポートベクトル回帰のアルゴリズムには，3つの評価関数 (kernel) が用意してあります．kernel='linear'，kernel='poly'，kernel='rbf' の3つです．linear は線形関数，poly は多項式関数，rbf は radial basis function と呼ばれます．

svr.py のプログラムでは，kernel='rbf' を採用しています．

svr.py
```
import pandas as pd
import numpy as np
from sklearn.svm import SVR
import matplotlib.pyplot as plt
import re,os
data=pd.read_csv('ice.csv')
x=data[['temp','street']]
y=data['ice']
clf=SVR(kernel='rbf',C=1e7,epsilon=.01,max_iter=-1,tol=1e-7,
    verbose=1,gamma=10.1).fit(x,y)
print(clf.score(x,y))
t=np.arange(0.0,31.0)
plt.plot(t,y,'--',t,clf.predict(x),'-')
plt.show()
```

実際に，svr.py プログラムを実行してみましょう．

`$ wget $take/svr.py` で svr.py をダウンロード，`$ python svr.py` コマンドで実行した結果が以下です．

```
[LibSVM]....*
optimization finished, #iter = 283
obj = -29835727003.934799, rho = -13666.666667
nSV = 31, nBSV = 1
0.969019753108
```
R-squared: 0.969019753108

機械学習では，通常，繰返しの学習が必要です．この場合，繰返し回数 = 283 で，システムが最適値に収束しています．R-squared 値 = 0.9690 であることが分かります．従来の統計手法に比べて（表 1.0 を参照），格段に R-squared 値が向上していることが分かります．

多くの重回帰アルゴリズムでは，R-squared 値が 0.45 付近で，分位点回帰アルゴリズムだけが 0.5757 と高く，SVR アルゴリズムがどれほど強力であるか分かります．

パラメータを変更して，R-squared 値がどのように変化するか確かめてみましょう．

2.1　カーネルリッジ回帰 KRR

サポートベクトル回帰 SVR に比べて，パラメータの設定は複雑ではありません．ここでは，評価関数 kernel='rbf', alpha=1e-8 と設定しています．カーネルリッジ回帰 KRR (Kernel Ridge Regression) アルゴリズムでは，KernelRidge ライブラリを呼び出します．alpha パラメータは，SVR アルゴリズムのペナルティパラメータ C の $((2*C)^{-1})$ に相当します．

カーネルリッジ回帰の機械学習モデル clf は，次のように定義しています．
`clf=KernelRidge(kernel='rbf',alpha=1e-8).fit(x,y)`

krr.py
```python
import pandas as pd
import numpy as np
from sklearn.kernel_ridge import KernelRidge
import matplotlib.pyplot as plt
data=pd.read_csv('ice.csv')
```

```
x=data[['temp','street']]
y=data['ice']
clf= KernelRidge(kernel='rbf',alpha=1e-8).fit(x,y)
print(clf.score(x,y))
t=np.arange(0.0,31.0)
plt.plot(t,y,'--',t,clf.predict(x),'-')
plt.show()
```

krr.py を実行してみましょう．`$ wget $take/krr.py` で krr.py をダウンロード，`$ python krr.py` コマンドで実行した結果は以下です．
R-squared: 0.984509772248

R-squared 値 = 0.9845 となり，この問題では，SVR よりも R-squared 値が向上していることが分かります．

2.2 ナイーブ・ベイズ sklearn.naive_bayes 機械学習

ナイーブ・ベイズのアルゴリズムは，広く使われている機械学習手法です．ナイーブ・ベイズには 3 つの評価関数があります．

1. GaussianNB
2. MultinomialNB
3. BernoulliNB

それぞれの評価関数の使い方を説明します．

ガウジアン・ナイーブ・ベイズ (GaussianNB) の機械学習モデル clf は，次のように定義します．
`clf=GaussianNB()`

naive_bayes.py
```
import pandas as pd
import numpy as np
from sklearn.naive_bayes import GaussianNB
import matplotlib.pyplot as plt
data=pd.read_csv('ice.csv')
```

```
x=data[['temp','street']]
y=data['ice']
clf=GaussianNB()
clf.fit(x,y)
print(clf.score(x,y))
t=np.arange(0.0,31.0)
plt.plot(t,data['ice'],'--',t,clf.predict(x),'-')
plt.show()
```

$ wget $take/naive_bayes.py で naive_bayes.py をダウンロードし，
$ python naive_bayes.py を実行すると，次の結果が得られます．
R-squared: 0.967741935484

ナイーブ・ベイズには，ガウジアン関数以外に，MultinomialNB の評価関数があります．MultinomialNB 機械学習モデル clf は次式で表現します．
clf=MultinomialNB(alpha=1e-3)

naive_bayesM.py
```
from math import *
import pandas as pd
import numpy as np
from sklearn.naive_bayes import MultinomialNB
import matplotlib.pyplot as plt
data=pd.read_csv('ice.csv')
x=data[['temp','street']]
y=data['ice']
clf=MultinomialNB(alpha=1e-3)
clf.fit(x,y)
print clf.score(x,y)
t=np.arange(0.0,31.0)
plt.plot(t,data['ice'],'--',t,clf.predict(x),'-')
plt.show()
```

$ wget $take/naive_bayesM.py で naive_bayesM.py をダウンロードし，
$ python naive_bayesM.py を実行すると，以下の結果が得られます．
R-squared: 0.967741935484

3つ目の評価関数が，BernoulliNB 関数です．BernoulliNB 機械学習モデル clf は，次式で表現します．
```
clf=BernoulliNB()
```

BernoulliNB を使う場合は，入力 x をそのまま使うのではなく，入力 x から特徴抽出して，その特徴抽出した x を入力として利用します．ここでは，RBFSampler 関数を使って，次の方法で，x から特徴抽出 x に変換します．
```
x=data[['temp','street']]
rbf_feature=RBFSampler()
x_features=rbf_feature.fit_transform(x)
```

RBFSampler 関数以外には，Nystroem 関数があります．Nystroem 関数は，RBFSampler 関数よりも計算時間がかかりますが，正確な結果を生み出します．

naive_bayesB.py
```python
import pandas as pd
import numpy as np
from sklearn.naive_bayes import BernoulliNB
from sklearn.kernel_approximation import RBFSampler
import matplotlib.pyplot as plt
data=pd.read_csv('ice.csv')
x=data[['temp','street']]
rbf_feature=RBFSampler()
x_features=rbf_feature.fit_transform(x)
y=data['ice']
clf=BernoulliNB()
clf.fit(x_features,y)
print(clf.score(x_features,y))
t=np.arange(0.0,31.0)
plt.plot(t,y,'--',t,clf.predict(x_features),'-')
plt.show()
```

$ wget $take/naive_bayesB.py で naive_bayesB.py をダウンロード．
$ python naive_bayesB.py を実行した結果は以下です．
R-squared: 0.967741935484

2.3 決定木分類器 DecisionTreeClassifier

決定木分類器のプログラムが，decisiontreeclass.py です．ビッグデータ分析において，出力（アイスクリームの売上げ）に対して，どの入力変数（最高温度，通行人数）が影響するのか，知りたいところです．実は，clf.feature_importances 関数は，出力に対しての入力変数の重要度を提供してくれます．

決定木分類器の機械学習モデル clf は，次式で定義しています．
clf= DecisionTreeClassifier().fit(x,y)

---
decisiontreeclass.py

```
import pandas as pd
import numpy as np
from sklearn.tree import DecisionTreeClassifier
import matplotlib.pyplot as plt
data=pd.read_csv('ice.csv')
x=data[['temp','street']]
y=data['ice']
clf=DecisionTreeClassifier().fit(x,y)
print(clf.score(x,y))
print(clf.feature_importances_)
t=np.arange(0.0,31.0)
plt.plot(t,data['ice'],'--',t,clf.predict(x),'-')
plt.show()
```

$ wget $take/decisiontreeclass.py で decisiontreeclass.py をダウンロードし，$ python decisiontreeclass.py で実行すると，結果は以下になります．

R-squared: 0.967741935484

feature_importances: [0.27586207 0.72413793]

R-squared=0.9677 となりました．feature of importances の結果は，[0.20689655 0.79310345] なので，通行人数のほうが4倍ほど最高気温よりも重要度が高いことを示しています．つまり，通行人数のほうが最高気温よりもアイスクリームの売上げに大きく関わっていることを示しています．

2.4 近傍法

ここでは，3 つの近傍法 (KNeighborsRegressor, KNeighborsClassifier, RadiusNeighborsClassifier) を紹介します。

まず，近傍法 KNeighborsRegressor の機械学習モデル clf は，次式で表現できます。

`clf=KNeighborsRegressor(n_neighbors=1)`

kneighborsreg.py
```
import pandas as pd
import numpy as np
from sklearn.neighbors import KNeighborsRegressor
import matplotlib.pyplot as plt
data=pd.read_csv('ice.csv')
x=data[['temp','street']]
y=data['ice']
clf=KNeighborsRegressor(n_neighbors=1)
est=clf.fit(x,y)
print(clf.score(x,y))
t=np.arange(0.0,31.0)
plt.plot(t,y,'--',t,clf.predict(x),'-')
plt.show()
```

$ wget $take/kneighborsreg.py で kneighborsreg.py をダウンロードし，$ python kneighborsreg.py を実行すると，結果は以下になります。
R-squared: 0.969019544495

近傍法 KNeighborsClassifier の機械学習モデル clf は次式で定義できます。
`clf=KNeighborsClassifier(n_neighbors=1)`

kneighborsclass.py
```
import pandas as pd
import numpy as np
from sklearn.neighbors import KNeighborsClassifier
import matplotlib.pyplot as plt
```

```
data=pd.read_csv('ice.csv')
x=data[['temp','street']]
y=data['ice']
clf=KNeighborsClassifier(n_neighbors=1)
est=clf.fit(x,y)
print(clf.score(x,y))
t=np.arange(0.0,31.0)
plt.plot(t,y,'--',t,clf.predict(x),'-')
plt.show()
```

$ wget $take/kneighborsclass.py で kneighborsclass.py をダウンロードし，$ python kneighborsclass.py を実行すると，結果は以下になります．
R-squared: 0.967741935484

近傍法の RadiusNeighborsClassifier 機械学習モデルは，次式で表現できます．
clf=RadiusNeighborsClassifier()

radiusneighbors.py
```
import pandas as pd
import numpy as np
from sklearn.neighbors import RadiusNeighborsClassifier
import matplotlib.pyplot as plt
data=pd.read_csv('ice.csv')
x=data[['temp','street']]
y=data['ice']
clf=RadiusNeighborsClassifier()
clf.fit(x,y)
print(clf.score(x,y))
t=np.arange(0.0,31.0)
plt.plot(t,y,'--',t,clf.predict(x),'-')
plt.show()
```

$ wget $take/radiusneighbors.py で radiusneighbors.py をダウンロードし，$ python radiusneighbors.py を実行すると，結果は以下になります．
R-squared: 0.967741935484

2.5 確率的勾配降下法 SGDClassifier

確率的勾配降下法SGDClassifier (Stochastic Gradient Decendent) ライブラリを呼び出して，機械学習します．ここでは今までと違って，確率的勾配降下法では入力 x を使わず，いったん入力 x から特徴抽出し，その特徴抽出したデータ (x_features) を入力とします．

入力 x から特徴抽出するために，RBFSampler ライブラリを用いて，次の2行で入力 x から特徴抽出します．x_features が機械学習の入力になります．
rbf_feature=RBFSampler(gamma=1,random_state=0,n_components=100)
x_features=rbf_feature.fit_transform(x)

確率的勾配降下法SGDClassifier の機械学習モデルは，次式で表現できます．
clf=SGDClassifier()

また，機械学習も，clf.fit(x,y) ではなく，clf.fit(x_features,y) になります．

sgdc_rbfk.py

```
import pandas as pd
import numpy as np
from sklearn.kernel_approximation import RBFSampler
from sklearn.linear_model import SGDClassifier
import matplotlib.pyplot as plt
data=pd.read_csv('ice.csv')
x=data[['temp','street']]
rbf_feature=RBFSampler(gamma=1,random_state=0,n_components=100)
x_features=rbf_feature.fit_transform(x)
y=data['ice']
f=open('r.txt','wb')
for i in x_features:
    f.write("%s¥n" % i)
clf=SGDClassifier()
clf.fit(x_features,y)
print(clf.score(x_features,y))
t=np.arange(0.0,31.0)
plt.plot(t,y,'--',t,clf.predict(x_features),'-')
plt.show()
```

$ wget $take/sgdc_rbfk.py で sgdc_rbfk.py をダウンロードし，$ python sgdc_rbfk.py を実行すると，結果は以下になります．
R-squared: 0.967741935484

x_features の中身を見るために，r.txt ファイルに x_features を書き込みました．
$ cat r.txt

```
[-0.11452019 -0.12133566 -0.03352861  0.04445778  0.06121587 -0.05802043
 -0.12811228  0.11121895 -0.08070618  0.09461688 -0.03419943  0.08024093
 -0.10302908 -0.11729209  0.12640437  0.12014127  0.12911127 -0.08331184
 -0.02300941  0.07107639 -0.07877799 -0.01480092  0.10946523  0.10616586
  0.08299858 -0.11605893  0.1343433  -0.00927928  0.13219732 -0.13326778
 -0.07692323  0.10848421  0.11425452  0.12738431  0.13673958 -0.06362843
  0.11725335 -0.11880683 -0.14132801  0.09127831  0.14048837 -0.08513745
  0.01049231  0.11298819 -0.12006165 -0.08852809 -0.04386115  0.03057302
  0.14070629  0.09414339  0.001754    0.12784243 -0.00276444 -0.01406361
 -0.0520591  -0.1061085  -0.06371916 -0.14003519  0.07782192  0.13599635
  0.14130975 -0.07018444 -0.05537761 -0.14132765  0.09767741  0.01796868
 -0.08805287 -0.09931217 -0.09853072  0.09699032 -0.13739015  0.06771632
 -0.11896407 -0.04865777 -0.13116109  0.05782747 -0.03402373  0.01533112
  0.13341881 -0.1302334   0.13757449 -0.13738225 -0.1187666   0.04174789
  0.1288596   0.13069097  0.06499096 -0.06764926 -0.13986773  0.02571267
  0.11407941  0.1414143  -0.02395985  0.10073036  0.01697214 -0.08222925
 -0.00777966 -0.09180965 -0.136419    0.02259354]
```
...

2.6　ディープラーニングニューラルネットワーク keras

　ここでは，ディープラーニングニューラルネットワーク (Neural-net deep learning) keras を紹介します．keras のライブラリを使うと，非常に簡単にニューラルネットを構築できます．人工ニューラルネットとは，多数のニューロンとそのニューロン間を接続するシナプス結合からなっています．最近で

は，さまざまなニューロンモデル，ニューラルアーキテクチャを簡単に構築できます．

本書では，一番簡単なアーキテクチャ，フィードフォワード型のニューラルネットを紹介します．フィードフォワード型とは，ニューロンの出力がフィードバックして自分の入力に入ってこないアーキテクチャのことです．

フィードフォワード型には，入力層，隠れ層，出力層の3種類があります．ディープラーニングという言葉を，最近はよく耳にしますが，隠れ層を多段にして，性能を向上させようという試みです．

knn.py
```
from keras.models import Sequential
from keras.layers.core import Dense,Activation,Dropout
from keras.optimizers import Adam
import pandas as pd
import numpy as np
from sklearn.metrics import r2_score
np.random.seed(100)
n_of_neurons=100
model = Sequential()
model.add(Dense(input_dim=2,output_dim=n_of_neurons,
   activation="relu"))
model.add(Dense(n_of_neurons,activation="relu"))
model.add(Dense(n_of_neurons,activation="relu"))
model.add(Dense(n_of_neurons,activation="relu"))
model.add(Dense(1))

adam=Adam(lr=1e-6)

data=pd.read_csv('ice.csv')
x=data[['temp','street']]
xnp=x.as_matrix()
y=data['ice']
ynp=y.as_matrix()

model.compile(loss='mse',optimizer='adam')
model.fit(xnp,ynp,nb_epoch=20000,verbose=1,shuffle=True)
#score=model.evaluate(xnp,ynp,verbose=0)
print("score: ",r2_score(ynp,model.predict_proba(xnp)))
```

kerasをインストールするには，次のpipコマンドを実行します．
```
$ pip install --upgrade keras
```
または，
```
$ sudo pip install --upgrade keras
```

kerasのOptimizersには次の7つのアルゴリズムがあります．Optimizersアルゴリズムの1つを使って機械学習します．

1. SDG(Stochastic gradient descent),
2. RMSprop (Root Mean Square Propagation：リカレントニューラルネット向き),
3. Adagrad (Adaptive gradient),
4. Adadelta (extension of Adagrad),
5. Adam (stochastic optimization),
6. Adamax (varient of Adam),
7. Nadam (Adam RMSprop)

kerasでは，Activations関数は，活性化関数あるいは伝達関数と呼ばれます．ニューロンの伝達関数には，次の8つの関数があります．

1. softmax,
2. softplus,
3. softsign,
4. relu,
5. tanh,
6. sigmoid,
7. hard_sigmoid,
8. linear

それぞれの伝達関数は，次のような関数です．

sigmoid関数 またはlogistic関数：$f(x) = 1/(1 + \exp(-x))$
tanh関数：$f(x) = \tanh(x)$.
softmax関数：$f(x) = 1/(1 + \exp(-\theta^{\mathrm{T}} x))$
softsign関数：$f(x) = x/(1 + |x|)$
softplus関数：$f(x) = \log(1 + \exp(x))$

relu (Rectified Linear Unit) 関数： $f(x) = \max(0, x)$
linear 関数： $f(x) = x$

　ニューラルネットモデル model は，Sequential() 関数で表現できます．また，それぞれの層の入力数，ニューロン数，出力数は，Dense コマンドで表します．

　また，ニューロンの伝達関数は，例えば，activation="relu"で設定します．model=Sequential() のコマンドで，空っぽの model を作成します．model.add コマンドで層を構築していきます．

　例えば，次のコマンドは，入力数が 2，出力数が 100，ニューロンの伝達関数は relu となります．

```
model.add(Dense(input_dim=2,output_dim=100,activation="relu"))
```

　次に隠れ層を追加するには，次の 2 行のコマンドで，100 個のニューロンを加えます．

```
n_of_neurons=100
model.add(Dense(n_of_neurons,activation="relu"))
```

　下の例 knn.py では，入力は 2，隠れ層が 3 層です．出力は 1 になります．

```
model = Sequential()
model.add(Dense(input_dim=2,output_dim=n_of_neurons,
 activation="relu"))
model.add(Dense(n_of_neurons,activation="relu"))
model.add(Dense(n_of_neurons,activation="relu"))
model.add(Dense(n_of_neurons,activation="relu"))
model.add(Dense(1))
```

　model.compile(loss='mse',optimizer='adam') のコマンドで，学習方法を Adam に設定します．

　adam=Adam(lr=1e-6) のコマンドで，学習率 (learning_rate) を 10^{-6} に指定しています．

　model.fit(xnp,ynp,nb_epoch=20000,verbose=1,shuffle=True) によって，epoch（学習回数）を最大 20000 回にしました．

　R-squared の値は，r2_score ライブラリで用いて計算しました．ニューロ

ン数や隠れ層数を変えると，実行結果も大きく変化します．

　$ wget $take/knn.py で knn.py をダウンロードし，$ python knn.py を実行すると，結果は以下になります．
('score: ', 0.63280994555500381)

　実行結果から，R-squared 値は，0.63 となっています．途中経過を見たくない場合は，verbose=0 にします．

---
keywords
伝達関数，ニューロン，入力層，隠れ層，出力層，epoch, Adam, r2_score, verbose

第3章

アンサンブル機械学習

　アンサンブル機械学習とは，複数の学習器を組み合わせて，学習能力を向上させる方法です．ここでは，Adaboost, Randomforest, ExtraTree, ExtraTrees, GradientBoosting, Bagging, 多数決分類器 (VotingClassifier) の7つの例を紹介します．

3.0　アダブースト (Adaboost)

　最初に紹介するのは，サポートベクトル分類器 (SVC) をアダブースト分類器 (AdaboostClassifier) でアンサンブルする学習法です．単純なSVC機械学習モデル (clf1) とSVC+アダブースト機械学習モデル (clf2) とを比較してみます．

```
clf1=SVC(probability=True,kernel='linear')
clf2=AdaBoostClassifier(SVC(probability=True,kernel='linear'),
n_estimators=100,learning_rate=1.0,algorithm='SAMME')
```

```
adaboostclass.py
import pandas as pd
import numpy as np
from sklearn.svm import SVC
from sklearn.ensemble import AdaBoostClassifier
import matplotlib.pyplot as plt
data=pd.read_csv('ice.csv')
x=data[['temp','street']]
```

```
y=data['ice']
clf1=SVC(probability=True,kernel='linear')
clf2=AdaBoostClassifier(SVC(probability=True,kernel='linear'),
  n_estimators=100,learning_rate=1.0,algorithm='SAMME')
clf1.fit(x,y)
clf2.fit(x,y)
p1=clf1.predict(x)
p2=clf2.predict(x)
print clf1.score(x,y)
print clf2.score(x,y)
t=np.arange(0.0,31.0)
plt.plot(t,data['ice'],'--b')
plt.plot(t,p1,':b')
plt.plot(t,p2,'-b')
plt.legend(('real','svc','adaBoost'))
#plt.plot(t,data['ice'],':b',t,p1,'-b',t,p2,'--b')
plt.show()
```

$ `wget $take/adaboostclass.py` で adaboostclass.py をダウンロードし，$ `python adaboostclass.py` を実行した結果は次のとおりで，アダブーストのアンサンブル学習をしても，R-squared 値は向上していません．しかしながら，重回帰手法に比べて，R-squared 値が著しく向上していることが分かります．

R-squared: 0.967741935484 (SVC)

R-squared: 0.967741935484 (Adaboost (SVC))

次に，決定木回帰 (DecisionTreeRegressor) をアダブースト手法でアンサンブル学習してみます．単純な決定木回帰学習モデル (clf1) と決定木回帰＋アダブースト学習 (clf2) は，次式で表現します．

`clf1=DecisionTreeRegressor(max_depth=4)`

`rng=np.random.RandomState(1)`

`clf2=AdaBoostRegressor(DecisionTreeRegressor(max_depth=4),`
`n_estimators=300,random_state=rng)`

adaboostreg.py

```
import pandas as pd
import numpy as np
import statsmodels.api as sm
from sklearn.tree import DecisionTreeRegressor
from sklearn.ensemble import AdaBoostRegressor
import matplotlib.pyplot as plt
data=pd.read_csv('ice.csv')
x=data[['temp','street']]
y=data['ice']
rng=np.random.RandomState(1)
clf1=DecisionTreeRegressor(max_depth=4)
clf2=AdaBoostRegressor(DecisionTreeRegressor(max_depth=4),
  n_estimators=300,random_state=rng)
clf1.fit(x,y)
clf2.fit(x,y)
p1=clf1.predict(x)
p2=clf2.predict(x)
print clf1.score(x,y)
print clf2.score(x,y)
t=np.arange(0.0,31.0)
plt.plot(t,data['ice'],'--b')
plt.plot(t,p1,':b')
plt.plot(t,p2,'-b')
plt.legend(('real','dtree','adaB'))
#plt.plot(t,data['ice'],':b',t,p1,'-b',t,p2,'--b')
plt.show()
```

$ wget \$take/adaboostreg.py で adaboostreg.py をダウンロードし，
$ python adaboostreg.py を実行した結果は以下です．
R-squared: 0.766011846555（決定木回帰）
R-squared: 0.9603546744（Adaboost（決定木回帰））

実行結果から，決定木回帰をアダブースト手法でアンサンブル学習すると，明らかに R-squared 値が向上することが分かります．

3.1 ランダムフォーレスト (RandomForest)

ランダムフォーレストという名前は，森が多くの木から成り立っていることから来ています．木の数は，n_estimators = 200 という具合に指定します．この場合，木の数 = 200 となります．面白いのは，木の数が多ければ R-squared 値が良くなるわけではないことです．最適な木の数があるようです．読者諸氏も，パラメータを変更して試してください．

ランダムフォーレスト RandomForest の機械学習モデル clf は，次式で表現できます．

clf=RandomForestClassifier(n_estimators=200, min_samples_split=1)

```
randomforestclass.py

import pandas as pd
import numpy as np
import statsmodels.api as sm
from sklearn.ensemble import RandomForestClassifier
import matplotlib.pyplot as plt
data=pd.read_csv('ice.csv')
x=data[['temp','street']]
y=data['ice']
clf=RandomForestClassifier(n_estimators=200, min_samples_split=1)
clf.fit(x,y)
print(clf.score(x,y))
print(clf.feature_importances_)
p=clf.predict(x)
t=np.arange(0.0,31.0)
plt.plot(t,data['ice'],'--b')
plt.plot(t,p,'-b')
plt.legend(('real','randomF'))
plt.show()
```

$ wget $take/randomforestclass.py で randomforestclass.py をダウンロード．$ python randomforestclass.py を実行した結果は次のとおりです．feature_importances は，前述のとおり，パラメータ変数 ('temp' と 'street') の出力に対する重要度を表しています．

R-squared: 0.967741935484 (RandomForest)

feature_importances: [0.37513273 0.62486727]

n_estimators=10 にすると，R-squared 値は下がりました．
R-squared: 0.935483870968 (RandomForest)
feature_importances: [0.36895996 0.63104004]

n_estimators を 200 より大きくしても，結果は変わりません．

3.2　エキストラツリー (ExtraTree)

エキストラツリー ExtraTree の機械学習モデル clf は，次式で表現されます．
`clf=ExtraTreeClassifier()`

extTreeClass.py
```
from math import *
import pandas as pd
import numpy as np
from sklearn.tree import ExtraTreeClassifier
import matplotlib.pyplot as plt
import re,os
data=pd.read_csv('ice.csv')
x=data[['temp','street']]
y=data['ice']
clf=ExtraTreeClassifier()
clf.fit(x,y)
print(clf.score(x,y))
print(clf.feature_importances_)
t=np.arange(0.0,31.0)
plt.plot(t,data['ice'],'--',t,clf.predict(x),'-')
plt.show()
```

$ wget $take/extTreeClass.py で extTreeClass.py をダウンロードし，
$ python extTreeClass.py を実行した結果は以下です．
R-squared: 0.967741935484 (ExtraTree)
feature_importances: [0.37931034 0.62068966]

3.3 エキストラツリーズ (ExtraTrees)

著者が最も気に入っているのが，エキストラツリーズ (ExtraTrees) のアルゴリズムです．エキストラツリーズアルゴリズムは，多くの場合，良い結果を出してくれます．エキストラツリー (ExtraTree) とはアルゴリズムが違うので気をつけましょう．

エキストラツリーズの機械学習モデル clf は，次式で表現できます．
clf = ExtraTreesClassifier(n_estimators=100, max_depth=None, min_samples_split=1, random_state=0)

extratreesclass.py

```
import pandas as pd
import numpy as np
from sklearn.ensemble import ExtraTreesClassifier
import matplotlib.pyplot as plt
data=pd.read_csv('ice.csv')
x=data[['temp','street']]
y=data['ice']
clf = ExtraTreesClassifier(n_estimators=100, max_depth=None,
   min_samples_split=1, random_state=0)
clf.fit(x,y)
print(clf.score(x,y))
print(clf.feature_importances_)
p=clf.predict(x)
t=np.arange(0.0,31.0)
plt.plot(t,data['ice'],'--b')
plt.plot(t,p,'-b')
plt.legend(('real','exrandt'))
plt.show()
```

`$ wget $take/extratreesclass.py` で extratreesclass.py をダウンロードし，`$ python extratreesclass.py` を実行した結果は以下です．
R-squared: 0.967741935484 (ExtraTree)
feature_importances: [0.36241379 0.63758621]

R-squared 値は，0.967741935484 になります．

3.4 グラディエントブースティング (GradientBoosting)

グラディエントブースティングアルゴリズムにはさまざまなパラメータがありますが，パラメータを微調整すると良い結果が出るときがあります．

グラディエントブースティング (GradientBoosting) 機械学習モデル clf は次式で表現します．
clf = GradientBoostingClassifier(n_estimators=1000, learning_rate=0.2,max_depth=1, random_state=0)

gradboostclass.py
```python
import pandas as pd
import numpy as np
from sklearn.ensemble import GradientBoostingClassifier
import matplotlib.pyplot as plt
data=pd.read_csv('ice.csv')
x=data[['temp','street']]
y=data['ice']
clf = GradientBoostingClassifier(n_estimators=1000,
   learning_rate=0.2,max_depth=1, random_state=0)
clf.fit(x,y)
print(clf.score(x,y))
print(clf.feature_importances_)
p=clf.predict(x)
t=np.arange(0.0,31.0)
plt.plot(t,data['ice'],':b')
plt.plot(t,p,'-b')
plt.legend(('real','gradboost'))
plt.show()
```

 $ wget $take/gradboostclass.py で gradboostclass.py をダウンロードし，$ python gradboostclass.py を実行した結果は以下です．
R-squared: 0.967741935484 (GradientBoosting)
feature_importances: [0.01054839 0.10416129]

3.5 バッギング (Bagging)

　バッギング BaggingClassifier 機械学習モデルを使って，KNeighborsClassifier 機械学習モデル (clf1) と KNeighborsClassifier+バッギング機械学習モデル (clf2) を比較します．それぞれのモデルは次式で定義します．
clf1=KNeighborsClassifier()
clf2=BaggingClassifier(KNeighborsClassifier(),n_estimators=300, max_samples=0.8, max_features=0.5)

```
bagging.py
import pandas as pd
import numpy as np
import statsmodels.api as sm
from sklearn.ensemble import BaggingClassifier
from sklearn.neighbors import KNeighborsClassifier
import matplotlib.pyplot as plt
data=pd.read_csv('ice.csv')
x=data[['temp','street']]
y=data['ice']
clf1=KNeighborsClassifier()
clf2=BaggingClassifier(KNeighborsClassifier(),n_estimators=300,
  max_samples=0.8, max_features=0.5)
clf1.fit(x,y)
print(clf1.score(x,y))
clf2.fit(x,y)
print(clf2.score(x,y))
p=clf1.predict(x)
q=clf2.predict(x)
t=np.arange(0.0,31.0)
plt.plot(t,y,':b')
plt.plot(t,p,'-b')
plt.plot(t,q,'--b')
plt.legend(('real','KN','bagging'))
plt.show()
```

　$ wget $take/bagging.py で bagging.py をダウンロードし，$ python bagging.py を実行した結果は以下です．

R-squared: 0.161290322581 (KNeighbors)
R-squared: 0.838709677419 (Bagging (KNeighbors))

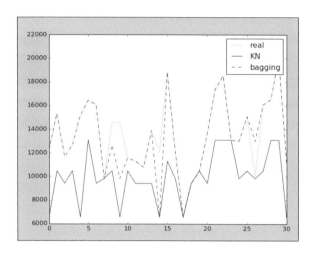

図 3.1　バッギング，KN，リアルデータとの比較

　ここで，KNeighborsClassifier() を KNeighborsClassifier(n_neighbors=1) に変えると，KNeighborsClassifier(n_neighbors=1) 分類器の結果は飛躍的に向上しますが，Bagging の手法では，KNeighborsClassifier(n_neighbors=1) 分類器の結果を向上できていません．

　`$ wget $take/bagging2.py` で bagging2.py をダウンロードし，`$ python bagging2.py` を実行した結果は以下です．
R-squared: 0.967741935484 (KNeighbors)
R-squared: 0.967741935484 (Bagging (KNeighbors))

　ExtraTrees の機械学習モデル (clf1) と ExtraTrees+バッギング機械学習モデル (clf2) を比較します．
`clf1=ExtraTreesClassifier()`
`clf2=BaggingClassifier(ExtraTreesClassifier(),n_estimators=300, max_samples=0.8, max_features=0.5)`

bagging_extratreesclass.py

```python
import pandas as pd
import numpy as np
import statsmodels.api as sm
from sklearn.ensemble import BaggingClassifier
from sklearn.ensemble import ExtraTreesClassifier
import matplotlib.pyplot as plt
data=pd.read_csv('ice.csv')
x=data[['temp','street']]
y=data['ice']
clf1=ExtraTreesClassifier()
clf2=BaggingClassifier(ExtraTreesClassifier(),n_estimators=300,
  max_samples=0.8, max_features=0.5)
clf1.fit(x,y)
print clf1.score(x,y)
p=clf1.predict(x)
clf2.fit(x,y)
print clf2.score(x,y)
q=clf2.predict(x)
t=np.arange(0.0,31.0)
plt.plot(t,y,':b')
plt.plot(t,p,'-b')
plt.plot(t,q,'--b')
plt.legend(('real','extraT','bagging'))
plt.show()
```

$ wget $take/bagging_extratreesclass.py で bagging_extratreesclass.py をダウンロードし，$ python bagging_extratreesclass.py を実行した結果は以下です．

R-squared: 0.967741935484 (ExtraTrees)

R-squared: 0.967741935484 (Bagging (ExtraTrees))

3.6 多数決分類器 (VotingClassifier)

多数決分類器は，アンサンブル学習をさらに向上させることができる有効な手法です．多数決分類器は次の方法で構築できます．

分類器 clf1, 分類器 clf2, ..., 分類器 clfN があるとすれば, 多数決分類器 (clf)

は，次のようなコマンドで N 個の分類器を使った多数決分類が可能になります．
```
clf=VotingClassifier(estimators=[('a1',clf1),('a2',clf2),...,
('aN',clfN)],voting='soft',weights=[2,1,...,5]).fit(x,y)
```

多数決分類器のライブラリ (VotingClassifier) は，次のコマンドで呼び出せます．
```
from sklearn.ensemble import VotingClassifier
```

ここで重要な役割を果たすのが，weights=[2,1,...,5] の重み関数です．分類器の重みを変えることで，多数決分類器の結果が大きく変わってきます．大きな数字ほど，その分類器の重みを大きくします．重みを考慮した多数決分類器は，重み付き多数決分類器と呼ばれます．

多数決分類器のプログラム概要を次に示します．
```
from sklearn.ensemble import VotingClassifier
clf1=Algorithm1
clf2=Algorithm2
     ⋮
clfN=AlgorithmN
clf=VotingClassifier(estimators=[('a1',clf1),('a2',clf2),...,
('aN',clfN)],voting='soft',weights=[2,1,...,5]).fit(x,y)
```

詳しい活用例は，4.1 節の "赤ワインの品質を判別できる人工ソムリエ" のところで説明します．

voting='soft' の場合，それぞれの分類器の平均予測確率を最大値にする計算に基づいて分類します．重み付き多数決分類器では，分類器を適切に構成したほうが正答率が向上するので，soft を選択します．voting='hard' の場合は，単純な多数決投票に基づいて計算します．

重みなし多数決分類器では，それぞれの特徴による多数決分類のための "strength of evidence" の違いを考慮せずに，すべての多数決の票に「同等」の重みを与えます．

重み付き多数決分類器では，それぞれの特徴による多数決分類のための "strength of evidence" の違いを考慮して，多数決の分類器の票に重みを与えます．

つまり，重み付き多数決分類器では，それぞれの分類器の相性を考慮していることになります．

多数決分類で使う分類器の性能が良いほど，多数決分類の性能は当然向上しますが，それだけでは不十分です．つまり，それぞれの分類器の特徴を生かしながら，多数決の重みを考慮して多数決分類すると，多数決分類器の正答率が飛躍的に向上します．

2016 年のリオ五輪での 400 m リレーで，日本は銀メダルを取りましたが，日本人の代表は 4 人とも 100 m の記録は 10 秒台です．ジャマイカ，米国などは全員が 9 秒台ですが，うまく選手の良さを引き出すリレー構成で，世界 2 位になれたわけです．リレーの場合は，バトンを渡す選手の順番も重要な要素になります．

まとめると，重み付き多数決分類器の場合，複数の弱い分類器を用意して多数決分類する場合，各分類器の投票に重みを考慮することで，飛躍的に多数決分類器の正答率を向上させることができます．

それぞれのアンサンブル学習の R-squared 値を，表 3.0 にまとめてみました．

表 3.0 アンサンブル機械学習と R-squared 値

アルゴリズム	R-aquared
SVC	0.96774
Adaboost(SVC)	0.96774
RandomForest	0.96774
ExtraTree	0.96774
ExtraTrees	0.96774
GradientBoosting	0.96774
KNeighbors	0.96774
Bagging(KNeighbors)	0.96774
ExtraTrees	0.96774
Bagging(ExtraTrees)	0.96774

第4章

アンサンブル機械学習の応用事例

ここでは，クレジットカードのデフォルトの学習事例と，赤ワインの品質を判別できる人工ソムリエの2つを紹介します．

4.0 クレジットカードのデフォルトの学習

クレジットカードのデフォルトに関する論文が，*Export Systems with Applications* 誌に出ています．論文のタイトルは，"The comparisons of data mining techniques for the predictive accuracy of probability of default of credit card clients" [0] です．

デフォルトとは，"支払期限を過ぎても最少額の未払いを引き起こした状態"のことを意味します．

早速，クレジットカードのデフォルトデータをダウンロードして試してみましょう．

http://archive.ics.uci.edu/ml/machine-learning-databases/00350/default%20of%20credit%20card%20clients.xls

[0] *Expert Systems with Applications* **36** pp.2473–2480 (2009).

default of credit card clients.xls ファイルは，エクセルファイルなので，次のプログラムで，xls フォーマットから csv フォーマットに変換します．

まず，ファイル名を default of credit card clients.xls から credit.xls に変えます．xls2csv.py ファイルをダウンロードして，credit.xls から credit.csv ファイルを生成します．

$ wget $take/xls2csv.py で xls2csv.py をダウンロードし，$ python

xls2csv.py を実行すると，credit.csv のファイルを生成します．

less コマンドで，credit.csv ファイルの中身を覗いてみます．

```
$ less credit.csv
```

"LIMIT_BAL","SEX","EDUCATION","MARRIAGE","AGE","PAY_0","PAY_2","PAY_3","PAY_4","PAY_5","PAY_6","BILL_AMT1","BILL_AMT2","BILL_AMT3","BILL_AMT4","BILL_AMT5","BILL_AMT6","PAY_AMT1","PAY_AMT2","PAY_AMT3","PAY_AMT4","PAY_AMT5","PAY_AMT6","default"

"20000.0","2.0","2.0","1.0","24.0","2.0","2.0","-1.0","-1.0","-2.0","-2.0","3913.0","3102.0","689.0","0.0","0.0","0.0","0.0","0.0","689.0","0.0","0.0","0.0","0.0","1.0"

...

xls2csv.py

```python
import xlrd
import csv
def csv_from_excel():
    wb = xlrd.open_workbook('credit.xls')
    sh = wb.sheet_by_name('Data')
    csv_file = open('credit.csv', 'wb')
    wr = csv.writer(csv_file, quoting=csv.QUOTE_ALL)
    for rownum in xrange(sh.nrows):
        wr.writerow(sh.row_values(rownum))
    csv_file.close()
csv_from_excel()
```

credit.csv ファイルから 2 つのファイルを作成します．テスト用のファイル credit_test.csv と学習用のファイル credit_train.csv の 2 つです．

まず，credit_test.csv ファイルを作ります．head -X file コマンドは file の先頭の行から X 行切り出します．head -1 file は，file の先頭の 1 行を表示します．

```
$ head -1 credit.csv >credit_test.csv
```

ファイルの中身を覗いてみましょう．

```
$ cat credit_test.csv
```

"LIMIT_BAL","SEX","EDUCATION","MARRIAGE","AGE","PAY_0","

PAY_2",”PAY_3",”PAY_4",”PAY_5",”PAY_6",”BILL_AMT1",”BILL_AMT2",”BILL_AMT3",”BILL_AMT4",”BILL_AMT5",”BILL_AMT6",”PAY_AMT1",”PAY_AMT2",”PAY_AMT3",”PAY_AMT4",”PAY_AMT5",”PAY_AMT6",”default"

23個の説明変数は，次のとおりです．

X1: クレジットの利用額

X2: 性別（1 = 男; 2 = 女）

X3: 教育（1 = 大学院; 2 = 大学; 3 = 高校; 4 = その他）

X4: 配偶者の有無（1 = 既婚; 2 = 未婚; 3 = その他）

X5: 年齢 (year)

X6–X11: 過去のペイメント

　X6 = 2005年9月

　X7 = 2005年8月

　⋮

　X11 = 2005年4月

　1 = 1か月遅延, 2 = 2か月遅延, …, 8 = 8か月遅延, 9 = 9か月遅延

X12–X17: 請求書額

　X12 = 2005年9月, X13 = 2005年8月, …, X17 = 2005年4月

X18–X23: 過去の支払額

　X18 = 2005年9月 X19 = 2005年8月, …, X23 = 2005年4月

X24：24個目が出力 (default payment:1 or 0) となります．

`tail -X file` コマンドは，file の最後の行から後ろ向きに数えて X 行を切り取ります．`>>` 記号は，ファイルにアペンド（付加）するコマンドです．つまり，次のコマンドは，credit.csv ファイルの最後の 100 行を credit_test.csv ファイルにアペンドするコマンドです．

```
$ tail -100 credit.csv >>credit_test.csv
```

したがって，credit_test.csv ファイルには，先頭の説明変数のラベルに 100 行のデータが付加されました．less コマンドで，ファイルの中身を覗いてみます．

```
$ less credit_test.csv
```

次に，head コマンドで，credit_train.csv ファイルを作成します．
```
$ head -29901 credit.csv >credit_train.csv
```

2つのファイル（credit_train.csv と credit_test.csv）の準備ができたので，ExtraTreesClassifier アンサンブル機械学習で早速，実験してみましょう．

credit_extratreesclass.py
```
from math import *
import pandas as pd
import numpy as np
from sklearn.ensemble import ExtraTreesClassifier
data=pd.read_csv('red.csv')
x=data[['fixed acidity','volatile acidity','citric acid',
  'residual sugar','chlorides','free sulfur dioxide',
  'total sulfur dioxide','density','pH','sulphates','alcohol']]
y=data['quality']
clf=ExtraTreesClassifier(n_estimators=82, max_depth=None,
  min_samples_split=1, random_state=0)
clf.fit(x,y)
test=pd.read_csv('red_test.csv')
x_test=test[['fixed acidity','volatile acidity','citric acid',
  'residual sugar','chlorides','free sulfur dioxide',
  'total sulfur dioxide','density','pH','sulphates','alcohol']]
y_test=test['quality']
print(clf.score(x,y))
print(clf.feature_importances_)
print(clf.score(x_test,y_test))
```

`$ wget $take/credit_extratreesclass.py` で credit_extratreesclass.py をダウンロードし，`$ python credit_extratreesclass.py` を実行すると，結果は以下になります．

R-squared: 0.999297658863 (ExtraTreesClassifier)
[0.06564034 0.01124482 0.03271751 0.02184793 0.06654127 0.09446342
  0.0507037 0.03607087 0.02924899 0.0281681 0.02998333 0.05022921

表 4.0 さまざまなアルゴリズムの R-squared 値の比較

アルゴリズム	R-squared
K-nearest neighbor	0.876
Logistic regression	0.794
Discriminant Analysis	0.659
Naive Bayesian	0.899
Neural networks	0.965
Classification trees	0.278
ExtraTreesClassifier	**0.9993**

0.04699753 0.04509691 0.04460779 0.04352465 0.04436174 0.04398287
0.04230672 0.04243047 0.04100851 0.04275595 0.04606736]
R-squared: 0.76（テストデータ）

ExtraTreesClassifier 機械学習能力は非常に高く，0.9993 になります．ほぼ 100 ％の学習の力です．

先ほど，紹介した論文の R-squared 値を本書の機械学習と性能比較してみましょう．圧倒的に，アンサンブル機械学習の ExtraTreesClassifier が一番性能が良いことが分かります．

テストデータ (x_test,y_test) に対する R-squared 値は，0.76 になります．

4.1 赤ワインの品質を判別できる人工ソムリエ

ここでは，赤ワインの品質を判別できる人工ソムリエを構築します．まず，赤ワインのデータが次のサイトにあります．
http://archive.ics.uci.edu/ml/datasets/Wine+Quality

入力の説明変数は 11 個あります．物理化学に基づく入力データには，以下のようなものがあります．

1. fixed acidity：不揮発性酸
   （tartaric acid 酒石酸：ワインの命 g/dm^3）
2. volatile acidity：揮発性酸
3. citric acid：クエン酸

4. residual sugar：残留糖分
5. chlorides：塩化化合物
6. free sulfur dioxide：遊離亜硫酸
7. total sulfur dioxide：総亜硫酸
8. density：密度
9. pH
10. sulphates：硫酸塩
11. alcohol：アルコール度数

赤ワインの出力（quality: 赤ワインの品質）は最後のコラムです．
12 quality: 赤ワインの品質は10段階にランク付けられています．

赤ワインのデータは下記サイトからダウンロードできます．
http://archive.ics.uci.edu/ml/machine-learning-databases/wine-quality/winequality-red.csv

先ほどのクレジットカードのデフォルトデータと同様に，学習用データ (red.csv) とテストデータ (red_test.csv) を作成します．まず，テストデータ (red_test.csv) を作成します．

```
$ head -1 winequality-red.csv >red_test.csv
$ tail -100 winequality-red.csv >>red_test.csv
```

次に，学習データ (red.csv) を作成します．

```
$ head -1500 winequality-red.csv >red.csv
```

赤ワインの重回帰式が述べられている面白いサイトがありました．
（出典：http://sudillap.hatenablog.com/entry/2013/04/27/203200）

ワインの味（グレード）
$$= 0.026 \times (酒石酸濃度) - 0.96 \times (酢酸濃度)$$
$$- 0.10 \times (クエン酸濃度) + 0.014 \times (残留糖分濃度)$$
$$- 2.3 \times (塩化ナトリウム濃度) + 0.0054 \times (遊離亜硫酸濃度)$$
$$- 0.0041 \times (総亜硫酸濃度) - 17 \times (密度) - 0.50 \times (pH)$$
$$+ 0.91 \times (硫酸カリウム濃度) + 0.26 \times (アルコール度数) + 22$$

6つのアンサンブル学習アルゴリズムを実験してみます．その6つとは，ExtraTrees, RandomForest, GradientBoosting, GaussianNB, KNeighbors, DecisionTreeの各アルゴリズムです．

red_extratreesclass.py

```python
from math import *
import pandas as pd
import numpy as np
from sklearn.ensemble import ExtraTreesClassifier
data=pd.read_csv('red.csv')
x=data[['fixed acidity','volatile acidity','citric acid',
  'residual sugar','chlorides','free sulfur dioxide',
  'total sulfur dioxide','density','pH','sulphates','alcohol']]
y=data['quality']
clf=ExtraTreesClassifier(n_estimators=82, max_depth=None,
  min_samples_split=1, random_state=0)
clf.fit(x,y)
test=pd.read_csv('red_test.csv')
x_test=test[['fixed acidity','volatile acidity','citric acid',
  'residual sugar','chlorides','free sulfur dioxide',
  'total sulfur dioxide','density','pH','sulphates','alcohol']]
y_test=test['quality']
print(clf.score(x,y))
print(clf.feature_importances_)
print(clf.score(x_test,y_test))
```

red_randomforestc.py

```
from math import *
import pandas as pd
import numpy as np
from sklearn.ensemble import RandomForestClassifier
data=pd.read_csv('red.csv')
x=data[['fixed acidity','volatile acidity','citric acid',
    'residual sugar','chlorides','free sulfur dioxide',
    'total sulfur dioxide','density','pH','sulphates','alcohol']]
y=data['quality']
clf=RandomForestClassifier(random_state=0,n_estimators=250,
    min_samples_split=1)
clf.fit(x,y)
test=pd.read_csv('red_test.csv')
x=test[['fixed acidity','volatile acidity','citric acid',
    'residual sugar','chlorides','free sulfur dioxide',
    'total sulfur dioxide','density','pH','sulphates','alcohol']]
y=test['quality']
p=clf.predict(x)
print(clf.score(x,y))
print(clf.feature_importances_)
```

red_gradboost.py

```
import pandas as pd
import numpy as np
from sklearn.ensemble import GradientBoostingClassifier
data=pd.read_csv('red.csv')
x=data[['fixed acidity','volatile acidity','citric acid',
  'residual sugar','chlorides','free sulfur dioxide',
  'total sulfur dioxide','density','pH','sulphates','alcohol']]
y=data['quality']
clf=GradientBoostingClassifier(n_estimators=82, learning_rate=0.1,
  max_depth=1, random_state=0)
clf.fit(x,y)
test=pd.read_csv('red_test.csv')
x=test[['fixed acidity','volatile acidity','citric acid',
  'residual sugar','chlorides','free sulfur dioxide',
  'total sulfur dioxide','density','pH','sulphates','alcohol']]
y=test['quality']
p=clf.predict(x)
print(clf.score(x,y))
print(clf.feature_importances_)
```

red_naive_bayes.py

```
import pandas as pd
import numpy as np
from sklearn.naive_bayes import GaussianNB
data=pd.read_csv('red.csv')
x=data[['fixed acidity','volatile acidity','citric acid',
    'residual sugar','chlorides','free sulfur dioxide',
    'total sulfur dioxide','density','pH','sulphates','alcohol']]
y=data['quality']
clf=GaussianNB().fit(x,y)
test=pd.read_csv('red_test.csv')
x=test[['fixed acidity','volatile acidity','citric acid',
    'residual sugar','chlorides','free sulfur dioxide',
    'total sulfur dioxide','density','pH','sulphates','alcohol']]
y=test['quality']
print(clf.score(x,y))
```

red_kneighborsclass.py

```
import pandas as pd
import numpy as np
from sklearn.neighbors import KNeighborsClassifier as kn
data=pd.read_csv('red.csv')
x=data[['fixed acidity','volatile acidity','citric acid',
  'residual sugar','chlorides','free sulfur dioxide',
  'total sulfur dioxide','density','pH','sulphates','alcohol']]
y=data['quality']
clf=kn(n_neighbors=13)
clf.fit(x,y)
test=pd.read_csv('red_test.csv')
x=test[['fixed acidity','volatile acidity','citric acid',
  'residual sugar','chlorides','free sulfur dioxide',
  'total sulfur dioxide','density','pH','sulphates','alcohol']]
y=test['quality']
print(clf.score(x,y))
```

red_decisiontreeclass.py

```python
import pandas as pd
import numpy as np
from sklearn.tree import DecisionTreeClassifier as dt
data=pd.read_csv('red.csv')
x=data[['fixed acidity','volatile acidity','citric acid',
   'residual sugar','chlorides','free sulfur dioxide',
   'total sulfur dioxide','density','pH','sulphates','alcohol']]
y=data['quality']
clf=dt().fit(x,y)
test=pd.read_csv('red_test.csv')
x=test[['fixed acidity','volatile acidity','citric acid',
   'residual sugar','chlorides','free sulfur dioxide',
   'total sulfur dioxide','density','pH','sulphates','alcohol']]
y=test['quality']
print(clf.score(x,y))
print(clf.feature_importances_)
```

以下のコマンドで，データ (red.csv, red_test.csv) と 6 つのアンサンブル機械学習プログラムをダウンロードします．

```
$ wget $take/red.csv
$ wget $take/red_test.csv
$ wget $take/red_decisiontreeclass.py
$ wget $take/red_extratreesclass.py
$ wget $take/red_gradboost.py
$ wget $take/red_kneighborsclass.py
$ wget $take/red_naive_bayes.py
$ wget $take/red_randomforestc.py
```

それぞれの R-squared 値の結果を次の表 4.1 に示します．

表 4.1　6 つのアンサンブルアルゴリズムと R-squared 値

アルゴリズム	R-squared
ExtraTrees	0.73
RandomForest	0.72
GradientBoosting	0.68
GaussianNB	0.64
KNeighbors	0.58
DecisionTree	0.48

ここで，3.6 節の 多数決分類器を使って性能向上を調べてみます．2 つのアンサンブル学習（ExtraTrees と RandomForest）を組み合わせてみます．voting1.py が多数決分類器のプログラムです．

voting1.py
```
import pandas as pd
import numpy as np
from sklearn.ensemble import ExtraTreesClassifier
from sklearn.ensemble import VotingClassifier
from sklearn.ensemble import RandomForestClassifier
data=pd.read_csv('red.csv')
x=data[['fixed acidity','volatile acidity','citric acid',
```

```
    'residual sugar','chlorides','free sulfur dioxide',
    'total sulfur dioxide','density','pH','sulphates','alcohol']]
y=data['quality']
clf2=ExtraTreesClassifier(n_estimators=82, max_depth=None,
    min_samples_split=1, random_state=0)
clf3=RandomForestClassifier(random_state=0,n_estimators=250,
    min_samples_split=1)
clf = VotingClassifier(estimators=[ ('et', clf2),('rf',clf3)],
    voting='soft',weights=[4,1]).fit(x,y)
test=pd.read_csv('red_test.csv')
x=test[['fixed acidity','volatile acidity','citric acid',
    'residual sugar','chlorides','free sulfur dioxide',
    'total sulfur dioxide','density','pH','sulphates','alcohol']]
y=test['quality']
print(clf.score(x,y))
```

$ wget $take/voting1.py で voting1.py をダウンロードし，$ python voting1.py を実行した結果は以下です．

R-squared: 0.74 (Voting1)

2つのアンサンブル学習を組み合わせると，R-squared 値が 0.73 から 0.74 に向上しました．

次は，3つのアンサンブル学習 (GaussianNB, ExtraTrees, RandomForest) の多数決分類器プログラム (voting2.py) です．

voting2.py

```
import pandas as pd
import numpy as np
from sklearn.naive_bayes import GaussianNB
from sklearn.ensemble import ExtraTreesClassifier
from sklearn.ensemble import VotingClassifier
from sklearn.ensemble import RandomForestClassifier
data=pd.read_csv('red.csv')
x=data[['fixed acidity','volatile acidity','citric acid',
    'residual sugar','chlorides','free sulfur dioxide',
    'total sulfur dioxide','density','pH','sulphates','alcohol']]
y=data['quality']
clf1=GaussianNB()
```

```
clf2=ExtraTreesClassifier(n_estimators=82, max_depth=None,
   min_samples_split=1, random_state=0)
clf3=RandomForestClassifier(random_state=0,n_estimators=250,
   min_samples_split=1)
clf = VotingClassifier(estimators=[('gnb', clf1), ('et', clf2),
   ('rf',clf3)], voting='soft',weights=[1,8,2]).fit(x,y)
test=pd.read_csv('red_test.csv')
x=test[['fixed acidity','volatile acidity','citric acid',
   'residual sugar','chlorides','free sulfur dioxide',
   'total sulfur dioxide','density','pH','sulphates','alcohol']]
y=test['quality']
print(clf.score(x,y))
```

$ wget $take/voting2.py で voting2.py をダウンロードし，$ python voting2.py を実行した結果は以下です．
R-squared: 0.75 (Voting2)

さらに，R-squared 値が 0.75 に向上しました．

次は，4 つのアンサンブル学習 (GaussianNB, ExtraTrees, RandomForest, KNeighbors) の多数決分類器プログラム (voting3.py) を試してみます．

voting3.py
```
import pandas as pd
import numpy as np
from sklearn.naive_bayes import GaussianNB
from sklearn.ensemble import ExtraTreesClassifier
from sklearn.ensemble import VotingClassifier
from sklearn.ensemble import RandomForestClassifier
from sklearn.neighbors import KNeighborsClassifier as kn
data=pd.read_csv('red.csv')
x=data[['fixed acidity','volatile acidity','citric acid',
   'residual sugar','chlorides','free sulfur dioxide',
   'total sulfur dioxide','density','pH','sulphates','alcohol']]
y=data['quality']
clf1=GaussianNB()
clf2=ExtraTreesClassifier(n_estimators=82, max_depth=None,
   min_samples_split=1, random_state=0)
clf3=RandomForestClassifier(random_state=0,n_estimators=250,
```

```
        min_samples_split=1)
clf4=kn(n_neighbors=13)
clf = VotingClassifier(estimators=[('gnb', clf1), ('et', clf2),
    ('rf',clf3),('kn',clf4)], voting='soft',
    weights=[1,8,2,1]).fit(x,y)
test=pd.read_csv('red_test.csv')
x=test[['fixed acidity','volatile acidity','citric acid',
    'residual sugar','chlorides','free sulfur dioxide',
    'total sulfur dioxide','density','pH','sulphates','alcohol']]
y=test['quality']
print(clf.score(x,y))
```

$ wget $take/voting3.py で voting3.py をダウンロードし，$ python voting3.py を実行した結果は以下になります．
R-squared: 0.76 (Voting3)

さらに，R-squared 値が，0.76 に向上しました．

次は，5つのアンサンブル学習（GaussianNB, ExtraTrees, RandomForest, KNeighbors, GradientBoosting）の多数決分類器プログラム (voting4.py) です．

voting4.py
```
import pandas as pd
import numpy as np
from sklearn.naive_bayes import GaussianNB
from sklearn.ensemble import ExtraTreesClassifier
from sklearn.ensemble import VotingClassifier
from sklearn.ensemble import RandomForestClassifier
from sklearn.neighbors import KNeighborsClassifier as kn
from sklearn.ensemble import GradientBoostingClassifier
data=pd.read_csv('red.csv')
x=data[['fixed acidity','volatile acidity','citric acid',
    'residual sugar','chlorides','free sulfur dioxide',
    'total sulfur dioxide','density','pH','sulphates','alcohol']]
y=data['quality']
clf1=ExtraTreesClassifier(n_estimators=82, max_depth=None,
    min_samples_split=1, random_state=0)
clf2=RandomForestClassifier(random_state=0,n_estimators=250,
```

```
    min_samples_split=1)
clf3=GradientBoostingClassifier(n_estimators=82,
   learning_rate=0.1,max_depth=1, random_state=0)
clf4=GaussianNB()
clf5=kn(n_neighbors=13)
test=pd.read_csv('red_test.csv')
x_test=test[['fixed acidity','volatile acidity','citric acid',
   'residual sugar','chlorides','free sulfur dioxide',
   'total sulfur dioxide','density','pH','sulphates','alcohol']]
y_test=test['quality']
clf = VotingClassifier(estimators=[('et', clf1), ('rf', clf2),
   ('gb',clf3),('gnb',clf4),('kn',clf5)], voting='soft',
   weights=[14, 3, 1, 1, 3]).fit(x,y)
print(clf.score(x_test,y_test))
```

`$ wget $take/voting4.py` で voting4.py をダウンロードし，`$ python voting4.py` を実行した結果は以下になります．
R-squared: 0.77 (Voting4)

さらに，R-squared 値が 0.77 に向上しました．

表 4.2 に示すように，Voting アルゴリズムで複数のアンサンブル学習を組み合わせると，R-squared 値が向上できることが分かります．

表 4.2　6 つのアンサンブルと Voting アルゴリズムの R-squared 値

アルゴリズム	R-squared
ExtraTrees	0.73
RandomForest	0.72
GradientBoosting	0.68
GaussianNB	0.64
KNeighbors	0.58
DecisionTree	0.48
Voting1 (ExtraTrees+RandomForest)	0.74
Voting2 (ExtraTrees+RandomForest+GradientBoosting)	0.75
Voting3 (ExtraTrees+RandomForest+GradientBoosting+GaussianNB)	0.76
Voting4 (ExtraTrees+RandomForest+GradientBoosting+GaussianNB+KNeighbors)	0.77

Votingの結果から分かることは，優秀なアルゴリズムだけの組合せが，必ずしもベストであるとは限らないことです．それほど優秀でないアルゴリズムでも，組合せによっては，優秀なアルゴリズムの組合せよりも良い成果が出る場合があります．

　人の特徴さえ抽出できれば，人間のチーム編成で応用できるかもしれません．

第5章

OpenCVと畳み込みニューラルネットワーク

　最近話題になっているのが，畳み込みニューラルネットワーク (Convolutional Neural Network:CNN) です．囲碁の世界でも，人工知能 (AlphaGo) が，ついに囲碁の世界チャンピオンに勝ちました．AlphaGo は最新の画像認識技術を基盤として構築されており，13層の畳み込みニューラルネットワークを使っています．また，3000万のサンプルを教師あり学習しています．13層の畳み込みニューラルネットワークが最適であるかどうか，現在のところ誰も分かりません．13層は，CPU や GPU をふんだんに使った試行錯誤の結果です．

　ここではまず，オープンソース画像処理ライブラリ，OpenCV を紹介します．5.0節では，写真画像から鉛筆画に変換する事例を紹介します．さまざまな最新の画像処理機能は，OpenCV 3.1.0 以降でないと利用できません．

　5.1節では，最新の画像認識技術の例として，有名画家の画風を絵画から特徴抽出し，写真画像を有名画家が描いたように画像変換します．

　Bash on Ubuntu on Windows 上で，GUI を使えるように必要なライブラリをインストールします．インストール方法を以下に記述します．

Bash on Ubuntu on Windows で GUI を実現する方法

　Windows 10 の Bash on Ubuntu on Windows 上で，GUI 機能を実現するには，次のステップに従ってインストールします．
1. vcxsrv-64.1.18.3.0.installer.exe ファイルを下記サイトからダウンロードします．
https://sourceforge.net/projects/vcxsrv/files/vcxsrv/1.18.3.0/vcxsrv-64.1.18.3.0.installer.exe

2. vcxsrv-64.1.18.3.0.installer.exe をダブルクリックし，Windows 10 にインストールします．

3. XLaunch をクリックします．

4. One large window を選んで，次へボタンをクリックします．次へボタンを押し続けて完了ボタンをクリックすると，XcXsrv Server が立ち上がります．

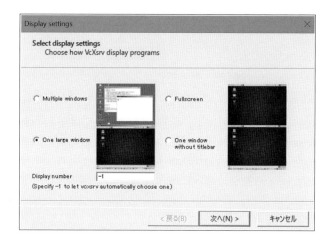

5. Bash on Ubuntu を立ち上げます．次のコマンドを実行して，必要なライブラリをインストールします．

```
$ sudo apt install ubuntu-desktop unity compizconfig-settings-manag
$ sudo apt install xfce4-session
```

次に，/etc/dbus-1/session.conf ファイルの設定が次のようになっているか確認します．必要があれば変更してください．
⟨listen⟩tcp:host=localhost,port=0⟨/listen⟩

6. 次の ccsm コマンドを実行して，デスクトップの機能を設定します．設定が終わったら Close ボタンをクリックします．

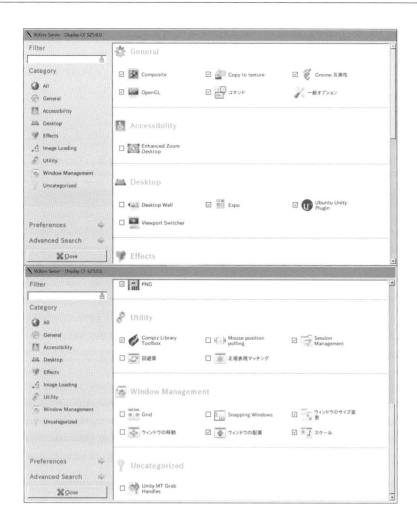

7. 次に，.bashrc ファイルに必要な設定を加えます．
```
$ cat .bashrc
cd
take='http://web.sfc.keio.ac.jp/~takefuji'
export DISPLAY=:0
alias x=xfce4-session alias desk='cd /mnt/c/Users/xxx/Desktop
```
　　　　　　　　　　　　　　※ xxx はユーザー名
```
alias home='cd /mnt/c/cygwin/home/yyy'
```
　　　　　　　　　※ yyy は Cygwin でのユーザー名
```
desk='/mnt/c/Users/xxx/Desktop'
```

次のコマンドで，Bash システムに，.bashrc ファイルの変更を認識させます．
```
$ source .bashrc
```

Bash で desk と入力すると，Desktop に移動できます．
```
$ desk
```

Bash からデスクトップにファイルをコピーしたい場合は，次のコマンドを実行します．
```
$ cp ccc $desk
```

8. 次のコマンドを実行し，xfce4-session を起動して，Bash の GUI を実現します．
```
$ xfce4-session または，x
```

設定がうまく行けば，次の画面が表示されます．

マウスの右ボタンをクリックすれば，すべてのメニューを表示します．

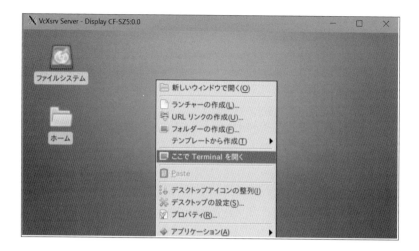

次の図では，Terminal を起動しました．

5.0 OpenCV と人工知能

　最新の OpenCV をインストールするのは少し複雑ですが，bashOn-Ubuntu_opencv.help ファイルにまとめてみました．コマンドなどを間違えないように実行するために，bashOnUbuntu_opencv.help ファイルからコマンドをコピー・アンド・ペーストしながら実行してください．

bashOnUbuntu_opencv.help ファイルをダウンロードします．

```
$ wget $take/bashOnUbuntu_opencv.help
```

bashOnUbuntu_opencv.help の中身閲覧は次のとおりです．

```
$ cat bashOnUbuntu_opencv.help
  $ wget https://github.com/Itseez/opencv/archive/3.1.0.zip
```
※ 76M ほどあります

```
  $ unzip 3.1.0.zip
```

次のコマンドを実行するには，1.3G ほどのスペースが必要になります．

```
$ sudo apt install build-essential libgtk2.0-dev libjpeg-dev
  libtiff4-dev libjasper-dev libopenexr-dev cmake python-dev
  python-numpy python-tk libtbb-dev libeigen3-dev yasm
  libfaac-dev libopencore-amrnb-dev libopencore-amrwb-dev
  libtheora-dev libvorbis-dev libxvidcore-dev libx264-dev
  libqt4-dev libqt4-opengl-dev sphinx-common
  texlive-latex-extra libv4l-dev libdc1394-22-dev
  libavcodec-dev libavformat-dev libswscale-dev default-jdk
  ant libvtk5-qt4-dev
$ cd opencv-3.1.0
$ mkdir build
$ cd build
$ cmake -D CMAKE_BUILD_TYPE=RELEASE -D
  CMAKE_INSTALL_PREFIX=/usr/local -D WITH_TBB=ON -D
  BUILD_NEW_PYTHON_SUPPORT=ON -D WITH_V4L=ON -D WITH_FFMPEG=OFF
  -D BUILD_opencv_python2=ON ..
$ make -j4
$ sudo make install
$ sudo sh -c 'echo "/usr/local/lib" >
  /etc/ld.so.conf.d/opencv.conf'
$ sudo ldconfig
$ sudo apt install execstack
$ cd /usr/local/lib
$ sudo execstack -c *.so
```

```
$ sudo execstack -c libopencv*.so.*
$ sudo ln /dev/null /dev/raw1394
```

インストールが完了したら，次のコマンドを実行して，OpenCV ライブラリをテストしてみます．

```
$ wget $take/cartoon.py
$ wget $take/yt.jpg
```

cartoon.py
```python
from PIL import Image
import cv2,sys
import numpy as np
import matplotlib.pyplot as plt
img = Image.open(sys.argv[1])
plt.imshow(img)
w,h=img.size
size=1
img.resize((w/size,h/size), Image.ANTIALIAS).save('small.jpg')
#img = cv2.imread('yt.jpg')
img = cv2.imread('small.jpg')
gray, out = cv2.pencilSketch(img, sigma_s=60, sigma_r=0.07,
   shade_factor=0.060)
cv2.stylization(img,gray)
cv2.imshow("cartoon",gray)
#cv2.imwrite(sys.argv[2],gray)
plt.show()
cv2.waitKey(0)
```

cartoon.py プログラムの中で，重要なコマンドが次の 1 行です．cv2 (OpenCV ライブラリ) の pencilSketch 関数を呼び出しています．パラメータを変えると鉛筆画が変化するので，いろいろ試してください．
```
gray, out = cv2.pencilSketch(img, sigma_s=60, sigma_r=0.07,
shade_factor=0.060)
```

次のコマンドを実行すると，私の顔が表示されるはずです．yt.jpg ファイルが入力の写真画像，t.jpg ファイルが生成される鉛筆画になります．
```
$ python cartoon.py jt.jpg t.jpg
```

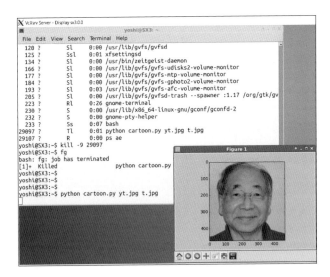

図 5.0　cartoon.py の実行の様子

表示された顔写真の閉じるボタンをクリックすると，次の鉛筆画が表示されます．

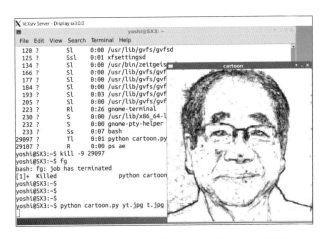

図 5.1　cartoon.py の実行結果の表示（鉛筆画）

カラー写真を変換する場合

cartoon_color.py
```
from PIL import Image
import cv2,sys
import numpy as np
import matplotlib.pyplot as plt
img = Image.open(sys.argv[1])
plt.imshow(img)
w,h=img.size
img.resize((w,h), Image.ANTIALIAS).save('small.jpg')
img = cv2.imread('small.jpg')
gray, out = cv2.pencilSketch(img, sigma_s=60, sigma_r=0.07,
   shade_factor=0.011)
cv2.stylization(img,out)
cv2.imshow("cartoon",out)
#cv2.imwrite(sys.argv[2],out)
plt.show()
cv2.waitKey(0)
```

カラーで変換する場合は，結構良い絵画になります（図 5.2〜5.4）．

```
$ wget $take/pexels-photo-28221.jpg [1]
$ wget $take/cartoon_color.py
$ python cartoon_color.py pexels-photo-28221.jpg [1]
```

[1] 図 5.3 はファイル名を city-road-street-buildings.jpg に，図 5.4 はファイル名を pexels-photo-137611.jpg に変えて変換したもの．

変換前

変換後

出典：https://static.pexels.com/photos/28221/pexels-photo-28221.jpg
creative commons

図 5.2　cartoon_color.py の実行結果

5.0 OpenCV と人工知能　　91

変換前

変換後

出典：https://static.pexels.com/photos/1440/city-road-street-buildings.jpg
creative commons

図 **5.3**　cartoon_color の実行結果（その 2）

変換前

変換後

出典：https://static.pexels.com/photos/137611/pexels-photo-137611.jpeg
creative commons

図 5.4 cartoon_color の実行結果（その 3）

5.1 畳み込みニューラルネットワークで絵画を生成

5.1 節では，最近流行の人工知能による，Art（絵画）製作の例を紹介します．畳み込みニューラルネットワークは，AlphaGo で利用されたことで世界的に有名になりました．ここでは，畳み込みニューラルネットワーク (Convolutional Neural Network:CNN) が，有名な画家の画風（特徴）を抽出し，写真画像にその画風を加えて，あたかも画家が画いたように絵画を生成します．

AlphaGo では，2 つの畳み込みニューラルネットワークを使っています．1 つは，try ("policy network") と呼ばれる，複数の候補を選択する畳み込みニューラルネットワークです．もう 1 つは，positions ("value network") と呼ばれる，次の手を評価する畳み込みニューラルネットワークです．"value network" は，MCTS (Monte Carlo tree search) のアルゴリズムを使っています．

畳み込みニューラルネットワークで，今までと違うところは，次の 3 つの特徴です．

1. 3D volumes of neurons（3D ニューロン郡）
2. local connectivity（受容野）
3. shared weights（共有重み付け）

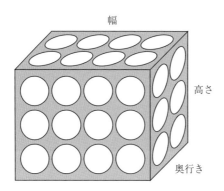

図 **5.5**　3D ニューロン郡

また，高速処理するために，従来のシグモイド関数の代わりに ReLU 関数 (rectified linear unit) を使います：$f(x) = \max(0, x)$．

$$f(x) = (1+e^{-x})^{-1} \quad （シグモイド関数）$$

max pooling 演算とは，次の図の場合，2×2 フィルタで最大値を選びます．

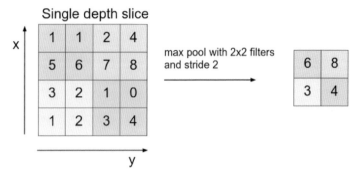

出典：http://cs231n.github.io/convolutional-networks/#pool

図 **5.6** Max pooling 演算例

Convolved feature では，次のビット演算を繰り返します．この場合，3×3 のフィルタとデータをビット演算します．

$$\text{filter} = \begin{bmatrix} 1 & 0 & 1 \\ 0 & 1 & 0 \\ 1 & 0 & 1 \end{bmatrix} \text{と data} = \begin{bmatrix} 1 & 1 & 1 \\ 0 & 1 & 1 \\ 0 & 0 & 1 \end{bmatrix} \text{をビット (AND) 演算すると，}$$

$\begin{bmatrix} 1 & 0 & 1 \\ 0 & 1 & 0 \\ 0 & 0 & 1 \end{bmatrix}$ になり，1 の数が合計 4 となります．

4 の右隣は，$\text{data} = \begin{bmatrix} 1 & 1 & 0 \\ 1 & 1 & 1 \\ 0 & 1 & 1 \end{bmatrix}$ なので，$\begin{bmatrix} 1 & 0 & 0 \\ 0 & 1 & 0 \\ 0 & 0 & 1 \end{bmatrix}$ の結果で 3 となります．

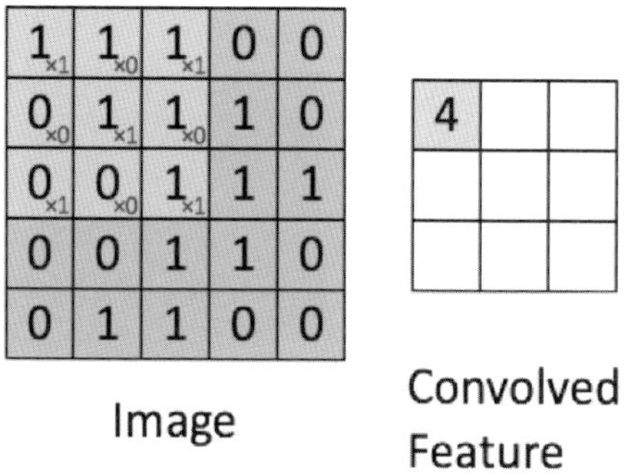

出典：http://cs231n.github.io/convolutional-networks/#pool

図 5.7 Convolved feature 演算例

本書では，さまざまなプログラムを紹介しましたが，ここで紹介するプログラムの終了には，高速のノートパソコンでも 4 時間ぐらいの実行時間がかかります．パソコンの CPU は i7 で，メモリも 8GB または 16GB 以上でないと，プログラム実行中に勝手に止まるかもしれません．

ここでは，深層ニューラルネットワークの chainer ライブラリを使ったプログラムを紹介します．その後に，keras ライブラリの例も示します．

chainer

まず，chainer ライブラリをインストールします．
```
$ sudo pip install chainer
```

次に，chainer-gogh.py ファイルをダウンロードします．
```
$ wget https://github.com/mattya/chainer-gogh/blob/master/chainer-gogh.py
```

models.py ファイルをダウンロードします．
```
$ wget https://github.com/mattya/chainer-gogh/blob/master/models.py
```

models.py が使う VGG_ILSVRC_16_layers.caffemodel(528M) が必要です．
```
$wget http://www.robots.ox.ac.uk/ṽgg/software/very_deep/caffe/VGG_ILSVRC_16_layers.caffemodel
```

この VGG_ILSVRC_16_layers.caffemodel は、"Very Deep Convolutional Networks for Large-Scale Image Recognition" の論文をベースに VGG チームが開発した 16 層の画像認識のためのモデルです。

[2] Copyright©2015, Eiichi Matsumoto.

The MIT License (MIT)

Permission is hereby granted, free of charge, to any person obtaining a copy of this software and associated documentation files (the "Software"), to deal in the Software without restriction, including without limitation the rights to use, copy, modify, merge, publish, distribute, sublicense, and/or sell copies of the Software, and to permit persons to whom the Software is furnished to do so, subject to the following conditions:

THE SOFTWARE IS PROVIDED "AS IS", WITHOUT WARRANTY OF ANY KIND, EXPRESS OR IMPLIED, INCLUDING BUT NOT LIMITED TO THE WARRANTIES OF MERCHANTABILITY, FITNESS FOR A PARTICULAR PURPOSE AND NONINFRINGEMENT. IN NO EVENT SHALL THE AUTHORS OR COPYRIGHT HOLDERS BE LIABLE FOR ANY CLAIM, DAMAGES OR OTHER LIABILITY, WHETHER IN AN ACTION OF CONTRACT, TORT OR OTHERWISE, ARISING FROM, OUT OF OR IN CONNECTION WITH THE SOFTWARE OR THE USE OR OTHER DEALINGS IN THE SOFTWARE.

chainer-gogh.py by mattya[2]

```
import argparse
import os,sys
import numpy as np
from PIL import Image
import chainer
from chainer import cuda
import chainer.functions as F
import chainer.links
from chainer.functions import caffe
from chainer import Variable, optimizers
from models import *
import pickle

def subtract_mean(x0):
    x = x0.copy()
    x[0,0,:,:] -= 120
    x[0,1,:,:] -= 120
    x[0,2,:,:] -= 120
    return x
def add_mean(x0):
    x = x0.copy()
    x[0,0,:,:] += 120
    x[0,1,:,:] += 120
    x[0,2,:,:] += 120
    return x

def image_resize(img_file, width):
    gogh = Image.open(img_file)
    orig_w, orig_h = gogh.size[0], gogh.size[1]
    if orig_w>orig_h:
        new_w = width
        new_h = width*orig_h/orig_w
        gogh = np.asarray(gogh.resize((new_w,new_h)))[:,:,:3].
            transpose(2, 0, 1)[::-1].astype(np.float32)
```

```
            gogh = gogh.reshape((1,3,new_h,new_w))
            print("image resized to: ", gogh.shape)
            hoge= np.zeros((1,3,width,width), dtype=np.float32)
            hoge[0,:,width-new_h:,:] = gogh[0,:,:,:]
            gogh = subtract_mean(hoge)
        else:
            new_w = width*orig_w/orig_h
            new_h = width
            gogh = np.asarray(gogh.resize((new_w,new_h)))[:,:,:3].
                   transpose(2, 0, 1)[::-1].astype(np.float32)
            gogh = gogh.reshape((1,3,new_h,new_w))
            print("image resized to: ", gogh.shape)
            hoge= np.zeros((1,3,width,width), dtype=np.float32)
            hoge[0,:,:,width-new_w:] = gogh[0,:,:,:]
            gogh = subtract_mean(hoge)
        return xp.asarray(gogh), new_w, new_h

def save_image(img, width, new_w, new_h, it):
    def to_img(x):
        im = np.zeros((new_h,new_w,3))
        im[:,:,0] = x[2,:,:]
        im[:,:,1] = x[1,:,:]
        im[:,:,2] = x[0,:,:]
        def clip(a):
            return 0 if a<0 else (255 if a>255 else a)
        im = np.vectorize(clip)(im).astype(np.uint8)
        Image.fromarray(im).save(args.out_dir+"/im_%05d.png"%it)

    if args.gpu>=0:
        img_cpu = add_mean(img.get())
    else:
        img_cpu = add_mean(img)
    if width==new_w:
        to_img(img_cpu[0,:,width-new_h:,:])
    else:
        to_img(img_cpu[0,:,:,width-new_w:])

def get_matrix(y):
    ch = y.data.shape[1]
    wd = y.data.shape[2]
```

```python
        gogh_y = F.reshape(y, (ch,wd**2))
        gogh_matrix = F.matmul(gogh_y, gogh_y, transb=True)/np.
                      float32(ch*wd**2)
    return gogh_matrix

class Clip(chainer.Function):
    def forward(self, x):
        x = x[0]
        ret = cuda.elementwise(
            'T x','T ret',
            '''
                ret = x<-120?-120:(x>136?136:x);
            ''','clip')(x)
        return ret

def generate_image(img_orig, img_style, width, nw, nh, max_iter,
  lr, img_gen=None):
    mid_orig = nn.forward(Variable(img_orig, volatile=True))
    style_mats = [get_matrix(y) for y in nn.forward(Variable
                  (img_style, volatile=True))]

    if img_gen is None:
        if args.gpu >= 0:
            img_gen = xp.random.uniform(-20,20,(1,3,width,width),
                      dtype=np.float32)
        else:
            img_gen = np.random.uniform(-20,20,(1,3,width,width)).
                      astype(np.float32)
    img_gen = chainer.links.Parameter(img_gen)
    optimizer = optimizers.Adam(alpha=lr)
    optimizer.setup(img_gen)
    for i in range(max_iter):
        img_gen.zerograds()

        x = img_gen.W
        y = nn.forward(x)

        L = Variable(xp.zeros((), dtype=np.float32))
        for l in range(len(y)):
            ch = y[l].data.shape[1]
```

```
                wd = y[1].data.shape[2]
                gogh_y = F.reshape(y[1], (ch,wd**2))
                gogh_matrix = F.matmul(gogh_y, gogh_y, transb=True)/
                              np.float32(ch*wd**2)

                L1 = np.float32(args.lam) * np.float32(nn.alpha[l])*
                     F.mean_squared_error(y[1], Variable(mid_orig[l].
                     data))
                L2 = np.float32(nn.beta[l])*F.mean_squared_error
                     (gogh_matrix, Variable(style_mats[l].data))/
                     np.float32(len(y))
                L += L1+L2

                if i%100==0:
                    print i,l,L1.data,L2.data

        L.backward()
        img_gen.W.grad = x.grad
        optimizer.update()
        tmp_shape = x.data.shape
        if args.gpu >= 0:
            img_gen.W.data += Clip().forward(img_gen.W.data).
                              reshape(tmp_shape) - img_gen.W.data
        else:
            def clip(x):
                return -120 if x<-120 else (136 if x>136 else x)
            img_gen.W.data += np.vectorize(clip)(img_gen.W.data).
                              reshape(tmp_shape) - img_gen.W.data

        if i%50==0:
            save_image(img_gen.W.data, W, nw, nh, i)

parser = argparse.ArgumentParser(
    description='A Neural Algorithm of Artistic Style')
parser.add_argument('--model', '-m', default='nin',
                    help='model file (nin, vgg, i2v, googlenet)')
parser.add_argument('--orig_img', '-i', default='orig.png',
                    help='Original image')
parser.add_argument('--style_img', '-s', default='style.png',
                    help='Style image')
```

```python
    parser.add_argument('--out_dir', '-o', default='output',
                        help='Output directory')
    parser.add_argument('--gpu', '-g', default=-1, type=int,
                        help='GPU ID (negative value indicates CPU)')
    parser.add_argument('--iter', default=5000, type=int,
                        help='number of iteration')
    parser.add_argument('--lr', default=4.0, type=float,
                        help='learning rate')
    parser.add_argument('--lam', default=0.0075, type=float,
                        help='original image weight / style weight
                            ratio')
    parser.add_argument('--width', '-w', default=435, type=int,
                        help='image width, height')
    args = parser.parse_args()

    try:
        os.mkdir(args.out_dir)
    except:
        pass

    if args.gpu >= 0:
        cuda.check_cuda_available()
        chainer.Function.type_check_enable = False
        cuda.get_device(args.gpu).use()
        xp = cuda.cupy
    else:
        xp = np

    if 'nin' in args.model:
        nn = NIN()
    elif 'vgg' in args.model:
        nn = VGG()
    else:
        print 'invalid model name. you can use (nin, vgg, i2v,
            googlenet)'
    if args.gpu>=0:
            nn.model.to_gpu()

    W = args.width
    img_content,nw,nh = image_resize(args.orig_img, W)
```

```
img_style,_,_ = image_resize(args.style_img, W)

generate_image(img_content, img_style, W, nw, nh, img_gen=None,
  max_iter=args.iter, lr=args.lr)
```

models.py（**VGG** のみ表示）

```
import chainer
from chainer import cuda
import chainer.functions as F
from chainer.functions import caffe
from chainer import Variable, optimizers

class VGG:
    def __init__(self, fn="VGG_ILSVRC_16_layers.caffemodel",
      alpha=[0,0,1,1], beta=[1,1,1,1]):
        print "load model... %s"%fn
        self.model = caffe.CaffeFunction(fn)
        self.alpha = alpha
        self.beta = beta
    def forward(self, x):
        y1 = self.model.conv1_2(F.relu(self.model.conv1_1(x)))
        x1 = F.average_pooling_2d(F.relu(y1), 2, stride=2)
        y2 = self.model.conv2_2(F.relu(self.model.conv2_1(x1)))
        x2 = F.average_pooling_2d(F.relu(y2), 2, stride=2)
        y3 = self.model.conv3_3(F.relu(self.model.conv3_2
            (F.relu(self.model.conv3_1(x2)))))
        x3 = F.average_pooling_2d(F.relu(y3), 2, stride=2)
        y4 = self.model.conv4_3(F.relu(self.model.conv4_2
            (F.relu(self.model.conv4_1(x3)))))
        return [y1,y2,y3,y4]
```

　ここで，テスト用の pekka.jpg と style_7.png（ゴッホスタイル）の画像ファイルをダウンロードします．

```
$ wget $take/pekka.jpg
```

https://github.com/mattya/chainer-gogh/raw/master/sample_images/style_7.png

すべて整ったら，次のコマンドを実行してみましょう．
```
$ python chainer-gogh.py -m vgg -i pekka.jpg -s style_7.png -o out -g -1
```

out フォルダに png ファイルが生成されます．

By courtesy of Dr. Pekka Neittaanmäki (Dean of the Faculty of Information Technology; Professor in Dept. of Mathematical Information Technology, University of Jyväskylä)

図 **5.8** 畳み込みニューラルネットワークによる演算結果 (lam=0.005)

すべての png ファイルを合成してアニメーション test.gif ファイルを作成してみます．imagemagick をインストールすると，複数の png ファイルから 1 つのアニメーション gif ファイルに変換してくれる convert コマンドが利用できます．
```
$ sudo apt install imagemagick
$ convert -delay 20 -loop 0 out/*.png test.gif
```

chainer-gogh.py プログラムの "–lam" の設定で変換が変わってきます．
"–lam" の値が小さいほど style 画像に近づき，大きな値では入力画像に近づきます．"–lr" の値は学習係数で，大きくすると当然，学習が速くなります．

keras

世界的に利用されている深層ニューラルネットワーク keras ライブラリの場合は，次のサイトから neural_style_transfer.py をダウンロードします．
https://github.com/fchollet/keras/raw/master/examples/neural_style_transfer.py[3]

keras ライブラリは次のコマンドでインストールできます．

```
$ sudo pip install -U keras
$ mkdir out
$ python neural_style_transfer.py pekka.jpg gogh.png out/out
```

実行させて，次のようなエラーが出る場合は，その次のコマンドを実行してください．

```
ImportError:No module named XXX.py
$ sudo pip install -U XXX.py
```

[3] Copyright©2015, François Chollet. All rights reserved.

Copyright©2015, Google, Inc. All rights reserved.

Copyright©2015, the respective contributors. All rights reserved.

The MIT License (MIT)

Permission is hereby granted, free of charge, to any person obtaining a copy of this software and associated documentation files (the "Software"), to deal in the Software without restriction, including without limitation the rights to use, copy, modify, merge, publish, distribute, sublicense, and/or sell copies of the Software, and to permit persons to whom the Software is furnished to do so, subject to the following conditions:

THE SOFTWARE IS PROVIDED "AS IS", WITHOUT WARRANTY OF ANY KIND, EXPRESS OR IMPLIED, INCLUDING BUT NOT LIMITED TO THE WARRANTIES OF MERCHANTABILITY, FITNESS FOR A PARTICULAR PURPOSE AND NONINFRINGEMENT. IN NO EVENT SHALL THE AUTHORS OR COPYRIGHT HOLDERS BE LIABLE FOR ANY CLAIM, DAMAGES OR OTHER LIABILITY, WHETHER IN AN ACTION OF CONTRACT, TORT OR OTHERWISE, ARISING FROM, OUT OF OR IN CONNECT

neural_style_transfer.py[3]

```python
from __future__ import print_function
from keras.preprocessing.image import load_img, img_to_array
from scipy.misc import imsave
import numpy as np
from scipy.optimize import fmin_l_bfgs_b
import time
import argparse

from keras.applications import vgg16
from keras import backend as K

parser = argparse.ArgumentParser(description='Neural style
        transfer with Keras.')
parser.add_argument('base_image_path', metavar='base', type=str,
                    help='Path to the image to transform.')
parser.add_argument('style_reference_image_path', metavar='ref',
                    type=str,
                    help='Path to the style reference image.')
parser.add_argument('result_prefix', metavar='res_prefix',
```

```python
                        type=str,
                        help='Prefix for the saved results.')

args = parser.parse_args()
base_image_path = args.base_image_path
style_reference_image_path = args.style_reference_image_path
result_prefix = args.result_prefix

# these are the weights of the different loss components
total_variation_weight = 1.
style_weight = 1.
content_weight = 0.025

# dimensions of the generated picture.
img_nrows = 400
img_ncols = 400
assert img_ncols == img_nrows, 'Due to the use of the Gram matrix, \
                    width and height must match.'

# util function to open, resize and format pictures into
  appropriate tensors
def preprocess_image(image_path):
    img = load_img(image_path, target_size=(img_nrows, img_ncols))
    img = img_to_array(img)
    img = np.expand_dims(img, axis=0)
    img = vgg16.preprocess_input(img)
    return img


# util function to convert a tensor into a valid image
def deprocess_image(x):
    if K.image_dim_ordering() == 'th':
        x = x.reshape((3, img_nrows, img_ncols))
        x = x.transpose((1, 2, 0))
    else:
        x = x.reshape((img_nrows, img_ncols, 3))
    x = x[:, :, ::-1]
    x[:, :, 0] += 103.939
    x[:, :, 1] += 116.779
    x[:, :, 2] += 123.68
    x = np.clip(x, 0, 255).astype('uint8')
```

```
        return x

# get tensor representations of our images
base_image = K.variable(preprocess_image(base_image_path))
style_reference_image =
  K.variable(preprocess_image(style_reference_image_path))

# this will contain our generated image
if K.image_dim_ordering() == 'th':
    combination_image
    = K.placeholder((1, 3, img_nrows, img_ncols))
else:
    combination_image
    = K.placeholder((1, img_nrows, img_ncols, 3))

# combine the 3 images into a single Keras tensor
input_tensor = K.concatenate([base_image,
                              style_reference_image,
                              combination_image], axis=0)

# build the VGG16 network with our 3 images as input
# the model will be loaded with pre-trained ImageNet weights
model = vgg16.VGG16(input_tensor=input_tensor,
                    weights='imagenet', include_top=False)
print('Model loaded.')

# get the symbolic outputs of each "key" layer (we gave them
  unique names).outputs_dict = dict([(layer.name, layer.output)
  for layer in model.layers])
# compute the neural style loss
# first we need to define 4 util functions

# the gram matrix of an image tensor (feature-wise outer product)
def gram_matrix(x):
    assert K.ndim(x) == 3
    if K.image_dim_ordering() == 'th':
        features = K.batch_flatten(x)
    else:
        features =
           K.batch_flatten(K.permute_dimensions(x, (2, 0, 1)))
```

```python
        gram = K.dot(features, K.transpose(features))
    return gram

# the "style loss" is designed to maintain
# the style of the reference image in the generated image.
# It is based on the gram matrices (which capture style) of
# feature maps from the style reference image
# and from the generated image
def style_loss(style, combination):
    assert K.ndim(style) == 3
    assert K.ndim(combination) == 3
    S = gram_matrix(style)
    C = gram_matrix(combination)
    channels = 3
    size = img_nrows * img_ncols
    return K.sum(K.square(S - C)) / (4. * (channels ** 2) *
        (size ** 2))

# an auxiliary loss function
# designed to maintain the "content" of the
# base image in the generated image
def content_loss(base, combination):
    return K.sum(K.square(combination - base))

# the 3rd loss function, total variation loss,
# designed to keep the generated image locally coherent
def total_variation_loss(x):
    assert K.ndim(x) == 4
    if K.image_dim_ordering() == 'th':
        a = K.square(x[:, :, :img_nrows-1, :img_ncols-1]
            - x[:, :, 1:, :img_ncols-1])
        b = K.square(x[:, :, :img_nrows-1, :img_ncols-1]
            - x[:, :, :img_nrows-1, 1:])
    else:
        a = K.square(x[:, :img_nrows-1, :img_ncols-1, :]
            - x[:, 1:, :img_ncols-1, :])
        b = K.square(x[:, :img_nrows-1, :img_ncols-1, :]
            - x[:, :img_nrows-1, 1:, :])
    return K.sum(K.pow(a + b, 1.25))
```

```
# combine these loss functions into a single scalar
loss = K.variable(0.)
layer_features = outputs_dict['block4_conv2']
base_image_features = layer_features[0, :, :, :]
combination_features = layer_features[2, :, :, :]
loss += content_weight * content_loss(base_image_features,
                                      combination_features)

feature_layers = ['block1_conv1', 'block2_conv1',
                  'block3_conv1', 'block4_conv1',
                  'block5_conv1']
for layer_name in feature_layers:
    layer_features = outputs_dict[layer_name]
    style_reference_features = layer_features[1, :, :, :]
    combination_features = layer_features[2, :, :, :]
    sl = style_loss(style_reference_features,
         combination_features)
    loss += (style_weight / len(feature_layers)) * sl
loss += total_variation_weight *
        total_variation_loss(combination_image)

# get the gradients of the generated image wrt the loss
grads = K.gradients(loss, combination_image)

outputs = [loss]
if type(grads) in {list, tuple}:
    outputs += grads
else:
    outputs.append(grads)

f_outputs = K.function([combination_image], outputs)

def eval_loss_and_grads(x):
    if K.image_dim_ordering() == 'th':
        x = x.reshape((1, 3, img_nrows, img_ncols))
    else:
        x = x.reshape((1, img_nrows, img_ncols, 3))
    outs = f_outputs([x])
    loss_value = outs[0]
    if len(outs[1:]) == 1:
```

```python
                grad_values = outs[1].flatten().astype('float64')
            else:
                grad_values = np.array(outs[1:]).flatten().
                                 astype('float64')
        return loss_value, grad_values

# this Evaluator class makes it possible
# to compute loss and gradients in one pass
# while retrieving them via two separate functions,
# "loss" and "grads". This is done because scipy.optimize
# requires separate functions for loss and gradients,
# but computing them separately would be inefficient.
class Evaluator(object):
    def __init__(self):
        self.loss_value = None
        self.grads_values = None

    def loss(self, x):
        assert self.loss_value is None
        loss_value, grad_values = eval_loss_and_grads(x)
        self.loss_value = loss_value
        self.grad_values = grad_values
        return self.loss_value

    def grads(self, x):
        assert self.loss_value is not None
        grad_values = np.copy(self.grad_values)
        self.loss_value = None
        self.grad_values = None
        return grad_values

evaluator = Evaluator()

# run scipy-based optimization (L-BFGS) over the pixels of the
  generated image
# so as to minimize the neural style loss
if K.image_dim_ordering() == 'th':
    x = np.random.uniform(0, 255, (1, 3, img_nrows, img_ncols))
        - 128.
else:
```

```
        x = np.random.uniform(0, 255, (1, img_nrows, img_ncols, 3))
            - 128.

for i in range(100):
    print('Start of iteration', i)
    start_time = time.time()
    x, min_val, info = fmin_l_bfgs_b(evaluator.loss, x.flatten(),
                                     fprime=evaluator.grads,
                                     maxfun=20)
    print('Current loss value:', min_val)
    # save current generated image
    img = deprocess_image(x.copy())
    fname = result_prefix + '_at_iteration_%d.png' % i
    imsave(fname, img)
    end_time = time.time()
    print('Image saved as', fname)
    print('Iteration %d completed in %ds' % (i, end_time
        - start_time))
```

付録

※ http://science.sciencemag.org/content/352/6293/1573.e-letters に掲載された論文

Black box is not safe at all.
by Yoshiyasu Takefuji

Before discussing the social dilemma of autonomous vehicles[1], we must remove all black boxes from any system for security reason.

The OBD-II specification is made mandatory for all cars sold in the United States since 1996. The European Union makes EOBD mandatory for all gasoline (petrol) vehicles sold in the European Union since 2001.

The OBD-II and EOBD specifications both contain black boxes where all car manufactures cannot full-test the black boxes. Besides, they have no security provided in the OBD-II and EOBD specifications. In other words, for more than fifteen years with neglecting security problems, we have been driving naked cars.

In the age of autonomous cars, we must reconsider such unsecure mandatory specifications. Why have we been forced to live with black-box testing without understanding the details of the black-box? We all know that black-box testing is not suitable for identifying the defects (hardware/software) in the black box.

However, open source is not automatically more secure than closed source[2]. The difference is with open source code you can verify for yourself (or pay someone to verify for you) whether the code is secure[2]. With closed source programs you need to take it on faith that a piece of code works properly, open source allows the code to be tested and verified to work properly[2]. Open source also allows anyone to fix broken code, while closed source can only be fixed by the vendor[1].

The open source hardware/software movement has been navigating us a good direction to get rid of all black boxes and to enhance security and incremental innovations.

References:

1. Jean-François Bonnefon, et al., The social dilemma of autonomous vehicles, *Science* 24 Jun 2016:Vol.352, Issue 6293, pp.1573-1576
2. http://www.infoworld.com/article/2985242/linux/why-is-open-source-software-more-secure.html

ブラックボックスは安全ではない
武藤佳恭

　自動運転車のソーシャルジレンマを議論する前に，我々はセキュリティ問題を考えるべきであり，世の中のシステムからすべてのブラックボックスをなくすべきです．

　1996年以降，米国内で販売されるすべての自動車は，OBDIIの仕様を満たさなくてはいけなくなりました．同様に，2001年以降，EUで販売されるすべてのガソリン車も，EOBDの仕様を満たさなければいけません．

　OBDIIやEOBDの仕様には，ブラックボックスがあるので，すべての自動車メーカーは，現在でも，そのブラックボックスの部分を完璧にテストできない状態にあります．

　さらに，OBDIIやEOBDには，セキュリティ機能がまったくありません．我々は，15年以上も，このセキュリティ問題を無視しながら，裸の車を運転しているわけです．

　自動運転の時代には，このセキュリティ問題を真剣に考え直す必要があります．ブラックボックスの詳細を知ることなく，ブラックボックスの中途半端なテストの状態で，車を運転してよいのでしょうか？ブラックボックス（ハードウェアやソフトウェア）の中に問題があった場合，ブラックボックステストが無意味であることは誰でも分かることですが……．

　かと言って，オープンソースが自動的にクローズソースよりも安全であるということは簡単に言えません．しかしながら，オープンソースであれば，少なくとも，我々自身が検証できます（あるいはお金を払って誰かに検証させる）．クローズソースでは，そのクローズソースコードが正しく動作することを祈るしかありませんし，オープンソースでは誰でも検証できる利点があります．オープンソースでは，もし問題があった場合，誰でもその問題のコードを訂正・修正できますが，クローズソースでは製造元でしか修正できません．

　オープンソース（ハードウェアやソフトウェア）の流れに従えば，ブラックボックス問題を解決できる可能性があるだけでなく，セキュリティを強化し，イノベーションを積み重ねることができます．

索引

【数字・欧文】

64 ビット OS, 3
Adaboost, vi, 51
Adam, 48
AI, iv
AlphaGo, vi, 81, 93
apt install, 13
apt search, 13
apt update, 9
apt upgrade, 9
apt-get autoremove, 14
apt-get install -f, 14
apt-get purge, 14
Bagging, vi, 58
BernoulliNB, vi, 35, 38, 40
cd, 5
chainer, vi, 95
CNN, 81, 93
Convolutional Neural Network, 93
Cortana, 2, 11
Cygwin, 3, 4
DecisionTree, 74, 75
DecisionTreeClassifier, vi, 15, 35, 41
df, 10
dpkg, 14
echo, 5
ElasticNet, v, 15, 32
epoch（学習回数）, 48
ExtraTree, vi, 55

ExtraTrees, vi, 56, 69, 75–78
fit() 関数, 19
GaussianNB, vi, 15, 35, 38, 72, 75–78
get-pip.py, 5, 6
GLS (Generalized Least Squares), v, 15, 24, 30
GLSAR, v, 15, 28, 30
GradientBoosting, vi, 57, 71, 75, 78
import, 18
keras, vi, 16, 35, 45, 103
KNeighbors, 73, 75, 77, 78
KNeighborsClassifier, vi, 15, 35, 42
KNeighborsRegressor, vi, 15, 35, 42
KRR (Kernel Ridge Regression), v, 15, 35, 37
Lasso 線形モデル, v, 15, 27, 30
Linux, 2
matplotlib, 22
MCTS (Monte Carlo tree search), 93
MixedLM (Mixed Linear Model), v, 15, 29, 30
MultinomialNB, vi, 35, 38, 39
nano, 5, 17, 20
numpy, 3, 7
OLS (Ordinary Least Square), v, 15, 17, 30
OMP 手法, v, 15, 31
OpenCV, vi, 81, 85

OpenCV 3.1.0, 81
OpenSSH, 4
pandas, 18
path, 6, 8
pip, 3, 5, 6
pip install, 7, 9, 13
pip list, 14
pip search, 14
pip uninstall, 14
plt.plot, 22
policy network, 93
positions, 93
pwd, 5, 10
Python, 3
Python-2.7.12, 3
QuantReg (Quantile Regression), v, 15, 30
r2_score 関数, 25
RadiusNeighborsClassifier, vi, 15, 35, 42, 43
RandomForest, vi, 54, 70, 75–78
ReLU 関数, 93
RLM (Robust Linear Model), v, 15, 25, 30
R-squared, 17, 20, 62, 75, 79
scikit-learn, 3, 7
scipy, 3, 7
SGDClassifier, vi, 15, 35, 44
source, 20
sudo, 9
SVR (Support Vector Regression), v, 15, 35, 36
tar, 10
try, 93
Ubuntu, 3
upgrade pip, 7
value network, 93
verbose, 49

vi, 4, 17, 20
Visual C++ 2008, 6
Visual C++ 2015, 6
VMware-workstation-player, 2
VotingClassifier, vi, 60
wget, 5
which, 6
Windows 10, 2
Windows 10 Anniversary Update, 3
WLS (Weighted Least Squares), v, 15, 24, 30

【あ行】

アダブースト, vi, 51
アンサンブル機械学習, 51
一般化最小二乗法, v, 15, 24, 30
イラスティックネット, v, 15, 32
エキストラツリー, vi, 55
エキストラツリーズ, vi, 56
オープンソース, iii, 81, 112

【か行】

確率的勾配降下法, vi, 15, 35, 44
隠れ層, 46
加重最小二乗法, v, 15, 24, 30
カーネルリッジ回帰, v, 15, 35, 37
機械学習, iii, 1, 15
機械学習器, 1
近傍法, vi, 15, 35, 42
グラディエントブースティング, vi, 57
グラフ線の色, 23
グラフ線の種類, 22
クレジットカードのデフォルト, 63
クローズソース, iii, 112
決定木分類器, vi, 15, 35, 41
混合線形モデル, v, 15, 29, 30

【さ行】

最小二乗法, v, 15, 17, 30
サポートベクトル回帰, v, 15, 35, 36
自己相関付き実行可能一般化最小二乗法, v, 15, 28, 30
重回帰式, v, 2, 17
重回帰分析, v, 16, 33
出力層, 46
人工ソムリエ, v, 67
人工知能, iv, 81, 85
深層ニューラルネットワーク, 95, 103
説明変数, 17

【た行】

多数決分類器, vi, 60
畳み込みニューラルネットワーク, vi, 81, 93
定数, 17
ディープラーニングニューラルネットワーク, vi, 15, 35, 45
伝達関数, 47

【な行】

ナイーブ・ベイズ, vi, 15, 35, 38
入出力関数 $y = f(x)$, 1
入力層, 46
ニューロン, 45

【は行】

バッギング, vi, 58
ビッグデータ, 15, 21
ビッグデータ解析, iv
ブラックボックス, 1
分位点回帰, v, 15, 30
分類器, 1

【ま行】

目的変数, 17
モデル構築, 2

【ら行】

ランダムフォーレスト, vi, 54
ロバスト線形モデル, v, 15, 25, 30

著者紹介

武藤佳恭（たけふじ よしやす）

慶應義塾大学工学部電気工学科卒業（1978），同大学院修士課程修了（1980），同大学院博士課程修了（1983）．工学博士（1983）．南フロリダ大学コンピュータ学科助教授（1983-1985），南カロライナ大学コンピュータ工学科助教授（1985-1988），ケースウエスターンリザーブ大学電気工学科准教授（1988-1996），tenured 受賞（1992）．慶應義塾大学環境情報学部助教授（1992-1997），同教授（1997-現在）．

研究：ニューラルコンピューティング，セキュリティ，インターネットガジェット．NSF－RIA 賞（1989），IEEE Trans. on NN 功労賞（1992），IPSJ 論文（1980），TEPCO 賞（1993），KAST 賞（1993），高柳賞（1995），KDD 賞（1997），NTT tele-education courseware 賞（1999），US AFOSR 受賞（2003），第 1 回 JICA 理事長賞，義塾賞（2015），Jyvaskyla 大学メダル授与．

著書：『武藤博士の発明の極意』（近代科学社）など 30 冊の本と 300 編以上の科学論文．

超実践 アンサンブル機械学習
© 2016　　Yoshiyasu Takefuji
　　　　　　　　　　　　　Printed in Japan

2016 年 12 月 31 日　初版第 1 刷発行

著　者　　武　藤　佳　恭
発行者　　小　山　透
発行所　　株式会社　近代科学社

〒162-0843　東京都新宿区市谷田町 2-7-15
電話 03-3260-6161　　振替 00160-5-7625
http://www.kindaikagaku.co.jp

加藤文明社　　　　　ISBN978-4-7649-0529-0
定価はカバーに表示してあります．